I0055468

RICH HABITS™

TONY MELVIN

Rich Habits

Published by
Melvin Media LLC
Florida
USA

tonymelvin.com

Copyright © 2017 Tony Melvin
All Rights Reserved.

No part of this book may be reproduced without the permission of the copyright owner.

General Disclaimer
The author and publisher expressly disclaim all and any liability to any person, whether a purchaser of this publication or not, in respect of anything and of the consequences of anything done or omitted to be done by any such person in reliance, whether whole or partial, upon the whole or any part of the contents of this publication.

Legal & Financial Advice
This publication is intended to give you legal or financial information based on the author's personal experience, it is NOT advice, and nothing on this publication should be considered legal or financial advice. The author is NOT a legal or financial advisor and no information is intended or may be construed as advice. Although the author uses his best endeavors to explain all relevant matters and instructions to you clearly, you may, however, misinterpret such explanations and/or instructions or you may omit to read all instructions. The author is not liable in any respect for any such misinterpretation or omissions. You have either received your own independent professional advice OR you have made your own deliberate decision not to obtain the relevant advice and you accept any risks of having done so.

Contents

1 - Introduction _____ 1

2 - The Missing Link _____ 7

3 - The Turning Point _____ 11

4 - The Problem with Money _____ 17

5 - Your Two Main Goals _____ 31

6 - The True Purpose of Debt _____ 53

7 - Your Solvency and Viability _____ 75

8 - How to Control Money _____ 83

9 - The Rich Continuum _____ 95

10 - The Laws of Allocation _____ 107

11 - Get Viable _____ 121

12 - Eliminating Killer Debt with the Solvency System _____ 129

13 - The Legal Game _____ 165

14 - Friend or Foe _____ 177

15 - Investing _____ 187

16 - Rich Habits Applied to Nations and Politics _____ 205

17 - My Story _____ 211

18 - The Rich Rebellion _____ 221

19 - Rich Habits Community & Coaching _____ 227

20 - Rich Habits Board Game _____ 231

21 - Rich Habits Pledge _____ 235

22 - Final Word _____ 237

23 - Rich Habits Definitions and Formulas _____ 239

24 - Rich Habits & Poor Habits _____ 243

25 - About the Author _____ 249

To my creditors who were so patient with me,

to my family and friends who supported me,

to my wife who stood by me and

to my son and daughters, the best parts of me.

1

INTRODUCTION

While the world of finance has become very complicated, you'll find this book refreshingly simple.

Contained in its pages is the missing link to your financial education. It answers a lot of questions and provides a clear road map to achieving your financial dreams.

No matter what you earn or how much debt you have, you can become financially free. You can become the master of your financial destiny.

The purpose of this book is to put you in the driver's seat on your road to wealth, and to provide you with confidence and certainty about your finances and your ability to create wealth—no matter what financial turmoil exists in the world.

The first thing to realize, about money, is that no real education exists on how to control it. If you take a look around, you'll see there are many individuals and companies who are having difficulty with this thing called "money."

Even politicians and world bankers can't get money

under control. They too are constantly struggling with the burden of debt and lack of money.

I think this is strange, that man, an intelligent species, capable of sending a man to the moon, and creating iPads, smartphones, and Tesla cars—still cannot get control over this thing called "money."

If after several attempts at driving a car, I was still unable to control it and kept crashing, I know I would come to the rather obvious conclusion: "I need to learn more about this thing called a car, so I can control it better."

Thankfully, there are plenty of people who can help me learn and understand a car, so I can control it better. However, where does one go to learn about money and how to control it?

And that, my friend, is the problem. The world is in the grip of a financial plague—it is *everywhere*. If you have ever found yourself in financial difficulty, overwhelmed with debt and hounded by debt collectors—or even less dramatic, just worried about how to pay off the mortgage —you have caught the plague. It's not your fault that money problems exist, because our whole society, every country, has the same plague; the plague of Poor Habits.

The Poor Habits Plague

According to Wikipedia, the Black Death was one of the most devastating pandemics in human history, resulting in the deaths of an estimated 200 million people and peaking in Europe in the years 1346 to 1353.

Apparently, it took roughly 200 years for the world's population to return to pre-plague levels. That was one hell of a plague!

Surprisingly, the solution was simple: Hygiene. Wash your hands, keep the streets clean, use running water, and kill the rodents. That was all it took.

Prior to the plague, people had poor hygiene habits. Once they understood that bacteria caused the plague, they developed simple hygiene habits that remain with us today as part of our modern culture.

What I find interesting about this historical event is that despite the devastating effects of the plague, the solution was easy to implement.

Once people understood what caused the plague, and they were able to control it, the plague ceased to exist.

The Poor Habits plague, which is rife throughout the world, might not be as deadly, but it can be just as devastating, and it is affecting far more people than the Black Plague ever did.

Thankfully, the solution is just as simple. All a person needs to do is understand what money is, how to control it, cease practicing Poor Habits and learn and apply Rich Habits.

Let me clarify what I mean by "Rich"—it means *plentiful or abundant*, and it comes from an old French word that means *powerful*. Notice it contains no mention of money, or a specific amount of money. Being rich means *having true abundance*—whatever that is for you. "Poor" on the other hand means *lacking sufficient money to live*, and you might think, at first glance, that the world is not in a grip of a Poor Plague and maybe I'm just overreacting. Well, why do people (and businesses and countries) continue to borrow money if they have enough to live?

The Solution

We have a very simple solution: learn what money is, cease practicing Poor Habits and start applying Rich Habits. Throughout this book, I will clearly identify both Poor and Rich Habits, for awareness of both is required, so you can first identify the *cause of the plague* and adjust your thinking and actions to avoid them and develop Rich Habits.

A word regarding habits: I don't believe habits must be broken, as this implies force, I believe habits are changed. When a person *understands* and can identify what is bad and what is good, they naturally choose the latter. Mankind doesn't need criticism or a whip to be decent; all Man needs is understanding.

Therefore, the first and most important Rich Habit is:

— RICH HABIT —

The Rich are aware of and practice Rich Habits.

— POOR HABIT —

The Poor are ignorant of Rich Habits and practice Poor Habits.

Your journey has begun, your "financial immune system" has been given a boost, and you are less likely to fall victim of the plague, for you know **Rich Habits exist.** Now let's get you on your way to being abundant, powerful and truly unstoppable.

— Rich Habits Free Community —

Throughout this book I make reference to the *Rich Habits Guidebook* and the *Rich Habits Toolkit*. The *Guidebook* contains step-by-step action plans that will help you apply the Rich Habits. The *Toolkit* contains spreadsheets, example letters, and other goodies promised in this book. Both are available as part of the *Rich Habits Free Community*, where you can also get help and support from others.

You can join for free at myrichhabits.com.

2

THE MISSING LINK

If you were holding a pen in your hand and let go, gravity would make it drop to the floor. We use gravity to get running water from a tap; and we defy it when we fly in an airplane. Understanding what gravity is, how it works and its different manifestations makes it possible to predict what is going to happen, to defy it or use its force for our own benefit.

And so it is with money.

Like gravity, money has certain laws; it behaves in certain ways and its power can be harnessed and controlled.

There are two very definite skills that need to be understood, known and applied when it comes to the subject of money.

First is the skill of *making money*. This vast subject is covered in numerous books; you can make money on the stock market, through property investing, and business, and through the countless different professions or jobs around the world. The ways to make money are immeasurable. While this book covers the investing aspects, it's not a detailed text on the subject of *making money*.

This book is about the other aspect of money: the skill of *controlling money*. This skill is by far the most important of the two. Many people around the world and plenty of businesses, no matter how much money they made, have fallen prey to the ignorance that surrounds the subject of money control. The whole basis of our worldwide economic turmoil has, at its roots, the mishandling of money.

I have met many people who are financially very well off. They have investments and decent incomes, yet despite all of this, they consider themselves on the edge of financial disaster. They are worried about the economy, their investments and their jobs (and who wouldn't when the media constantly reminds you to be worried?). It's a sad fact that there are some people who, despite their wealth, are in such fear of losing it, they can't enjoy it.

What I've discovered, however, is when these people learn what money is and the basic Rich Habits, they become very calm and certain about their situation. Their concerns seem to disappear once they have an understanding of money and how to control it.

Through helping many people, from the "rich" to the "not so rich," I have discovered this fact: *The skill of controlling money is the missing link.*

It doesn't matter how much money you make or have; if you fail to control it and fail to develop Rich Habits, you can get into trouble.

I know people who have followed the advice of a friend

or professional and lost money, yet understanding and following the Rich Habits would have prevented that from happening.

The less money you make, the more important it is to control money well. The more money you make, the more mistakes you can get away with, but if you continue to abuse money and violate the Rich Habits, you are heading for disaster; you crash just as hard from a financial high as you would from a plane crash. Like the violation of the law of gravity, violation of the Rich Habits can bring you down.

This brings us to another Rich Habit:

— RICH HABIT —

The Rich know there are two money skills: One is the ability to *make money* and the other is the ability to *control money*. The Rich know that control is the most important of the two.

— POOR HABIT —

The Poor focus on making money and rarely develop the ability to control it.

Understanding gravity has enabled Man to fly to the moon and beyond. If people understood money and practiced the Rich Habits, it would be possible to achieve prosperity for one and all, creating a world where everyone could reach the stars or achieve their dreams and desires.

Economical salvation does not occur from financial handouts, it happens by each individual in society understanding the Rich Habits and following them.

The salvation of a country's economy lies with the individual. It is the individual who can do something about the global financial situation by building a solid financial foundation for themselves and their family. With such a foundation, they can reach out and help their fellow Man do the same.

However, if you don't have that solid financial foundation, it is difficult to help others. I know, because I was once in complete financial despair, riddled with debt and ignorant of the Rich Habits. But one phone call changed it all.

3

THE TURNING POINT

△

It was around two o'clock when my phone rang.

"Hello, Mr. Anthony Melvin?" a serious voice asked.

"Yes," I answered.

"This is Sol Licit from *Harass & Partners*. I'm calling to inform you that if you don't pay your debt to Company X by the close of business today, we're going to continue with legal proceedings against you."

"Close of business? You mean five o'clock today?" I asked somewhat surprised as I checked the time.

"Yes, that's correct," he said coldly.

"Well, what does that mean: 'Continue with legal proceedings'? Are you going to make me go bankrupt?" I asked.

"If you don't pay by close of business today, then yes, we will take proceedings against you," he replied.

This didn't make any sense to me. Why would they force me into bankruptcy when I'd fully explained my situation? They knew I had no assets. So I replied, "I've already explained in my letters that I don't actually have any money or any assets for you to take because, if I did, I would simply sell those assets and pay you. The reason I'm not paying is because I don't have any money, so sending me into bankruptcy seems like a waste of time because you're still not going to get anything and neither is your client."

"Well, Mr. Melvin, you have until five o'clock today to pay the $3,575," and he hung up.

I thought, "This is really strange!" That day I was at a video editing studio helping with the final cut of a marketing video for a property group I was working with. While the editing process continued, I had some time to myself. I sat and thought for a while: "Why is this lawyer ringing me when I've been sending letters every week explaining my situation and what I'm doing?" Most of my creditors were quite happy with my plans. None had responded in this way and I owed more money to other creditors, way more in fact. Then I realized—with all the creditors who were happy with me, no legal firm was involved. I guessed that Company X had probably not received any of my letters or faxes as I had been sending them via their legal firm, *Harass & Partners*. I had a hunch that the lawyers were keeping my letters to themselves.

And so my story begins.

At this point in my life, I was over $300,000 in debt. I had sold all my assets (even my surfboard!) to pay off what I could. The car I was driving was a 10-year-old Ford, which my parents had lent me. As desperate as I was, I was determined to pay back my creditors.

I can tell you now that I achieved my goal. It wasn't

easy but I did it. In this book, I will show you how I went about handling creditors, paid back the debt and kept myself from going bankrupt.

I want to point out that while I will show you how to get out of debt, that is not the sole purpose of this book. To write a book that teaches you to "get out of debt" would not be a very good book because the focus is on a negative goal. It's a bit like having the goal to "not be sick." With such a goal, you are focusing on "sickness" and then trying to avoid it. You are constantly reminding yourself of the very thing you want to avoid. It is much more effective to focus on something you want to achieve.

Positive Goals & Negative Goals

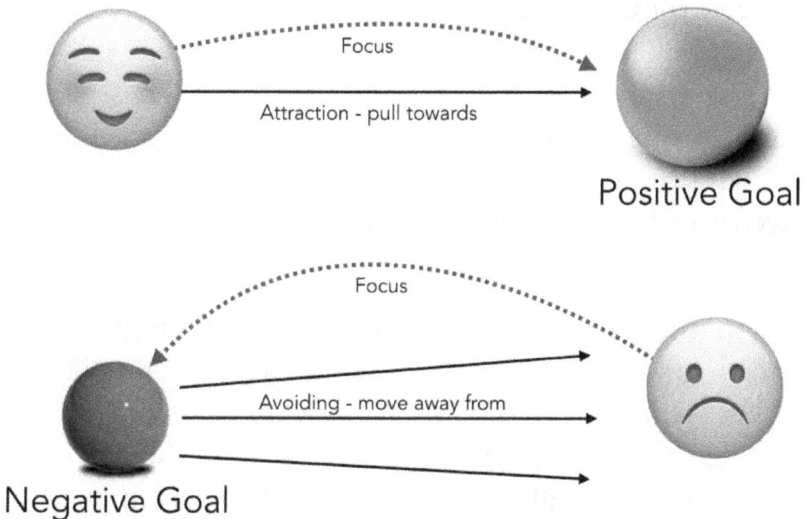

Focus

Attraction - pull towards

Positive Goal

Focus

Avoiding - move away from

Negative Goal

The goal of "being healthy" is much better and very different to the goal of "not being sick." Likewise, a goal of "being debt-free" means you have to think of "debt" and then think of being "free." It is much better to focus on a positive goal of "being rich." So, while this book will show you ways to get out of financial difficulty, my main endeavor is to teach you the Rich Habits so you can control your money and improve your wealth for the long term.

As for Sol from *Harass & Partners* (yes they're made up names; I've done that to protect the guilty!), I managed to avoid any legal proceedings. In fact, that phone call was the turning point for me. It resulted in no further legal action or harassment.

From that moment on, I realized I was on the way up. And even though I had more than a quarter of a million dollars of debt and absolutely no assets, I actually felt good about the whole situation, for the first time. The lessons I learned through walking this road allowed me to not only avoid bankruptcy and maintain my credit rating, they also allowed me to truly prosper. These are the lessons I will share with you.

No matter where you are right now, no matter what financial turmoil exists around you, no matter what you have lost, you can build yourself back up by realizing there is a way and *you can do it*. If you do, if you apply what I've written here, you will not only make it but this time, you'll be stronger than ever before because of your experience.

I wrote this book for you, to help you get out of your financial rut and build a solid financial foundation that you, your family, your friends and your community can enjoy.

It all starts with understanding what money really is …

4

THE PROBLEM WITH MONEY

Some say "money makes the world go round," implying that it is vitally important. Others believe "money is the root of all evil." Such contradicting ideas provide proof that money is a rather misunderstood subject.

Everyone from the humble street cleaner to whole nations are affected by the ignorance of this vital aspect of our existence. Despite man's advances in other fields of endeavor, we still have economic turmoil with individuals, large companies and whole countries going bankrupt or suffering financial difficulty. This is akin to getting an electrical shock regularly in your home because even though we use it, we still haven't quite figured out how electricity works. While I don't know the exact statistics, it's a safe guess that there are more people suffering from money problems than electric shock burns. Electricity is under control in most households and in companies around the world, but money is not.

And yet the subject of controlling money is not taught in school. Math, physics and chemistry might be taught, but the subject of "controlling money" is rarely taught.

Every child currently at school will sooner or later start

handling money, if they haven't already. We don't let people fiddle with electric wires unless they have been trained on the subject; that is, we don't let someone handle raw electricity unless they *understand* it and *can control* it. The same care and education should be applied to the subject of money because if it can ruin people's lives, bankrupt a company and wipe out whole economies, then I think it's just as dangerous as electricity—don't you?

Therefore, understanding what money is should be included in any child's education.

If you missed out on this education, let's start at the beginning and get a firm grasp of this thing called "money," so you can control it effectively.

If you have money handy, pull some out now and have a good look at the different values of notes and coins.

Let me ask you this question: Why is it that they are valued differently? Why, for example, is a $5 note worth less than a $20 note? Is it because of the size? Is it because it has a different drawing on it? Obviously not. Then why are they valued differently?

When I do this during a live event, someone will usually pipe up and say, "It's because we agree they are worth that much!"

And that is the first thing to know about money. Its value is based on an agreement.

— RICH HABIT —

The Rich know that the value of money is based solely on an agreement.

— POOR HABIT —

The Poor value money based on time.

The only reason you will accept a piece of paper or coins with funny pictures on them as payment for goods or services is because you know that everyone else has agreed to accept the same piece of paper or coins.

You are *certain* you can take that money and exchange it for something you need. You know the guy at the local shop will accept that money as payment for milk. You know and believe it. Everybody has agreed.

If suddenly everyone you met refused to accept your cash as payment and wanted something else, then your cash would become worthless. You would not use it anymore.

Because we all agree, money holds its value—or does it?

Have you ever made an agreement with someone and then after a little while, the agreement changed a bit? Then some time later it changed again. This happens all the time in human relationships. The one thing you know for certain is things will change!

Changing prices, giving items away for free that were once expensive, printing money with no assets backing it—all these changes combine into a twisted web that alters the agreement of what money is worth. And this brings us to our next lesson on this subject.

— RICH HABIT —

The Rich know that the value of money can be manipulated.

— POOR HABIT —

The Poor are oblivious to and victimized by money manipulation.

Those in power who control vast sums of money can change the value of share prices and move currencies up and down. In short, they can create false values that are too high or too low. Explaining how this happens makes for good party talk, but it serves no purpose to discuss it here other than to know that it does happen: The value of money gets manipulated.

Proof of this lies in the fact that inflation continues to occur despite all apparent efforts to stop it. The effects of inflation are quite often misunderstood. So, let's explore this briefly so you know what it is and how it affects you and your finances.

Effect of Inflation

Let's say an apple costs $1.

If inflation was 4% per year, the apple will cost you $1.04 in a year's time. If inflation continued at this rate, it would take 19 years for the cost of an apple to double.

Inflation at 4%

Year	Cost of an Apple	Year	Cost of an Apple
1	$1.00	11	$1.48
2	$1.04	12	$1.54
3	$1.08	13	$1.60
4	$1.12	14	$1.67
5	$1.17	15	$1.73
6	$1.22	16	$1.80
7	$1.27	17	$1.87
8	$1.32	18	$1.95
9	$1.37	19	$2.03
10	$1.42	20	$2.11

Inflation is described as an increase in prices, but it is actually a *decrease* in the value of your money. Using the example above, an apple would cost just over $2 in 19 year's time. Or to put it another way, if you only had $1, you could now only buy *half* an apple.

Cost of an Apple with 4% Inflation

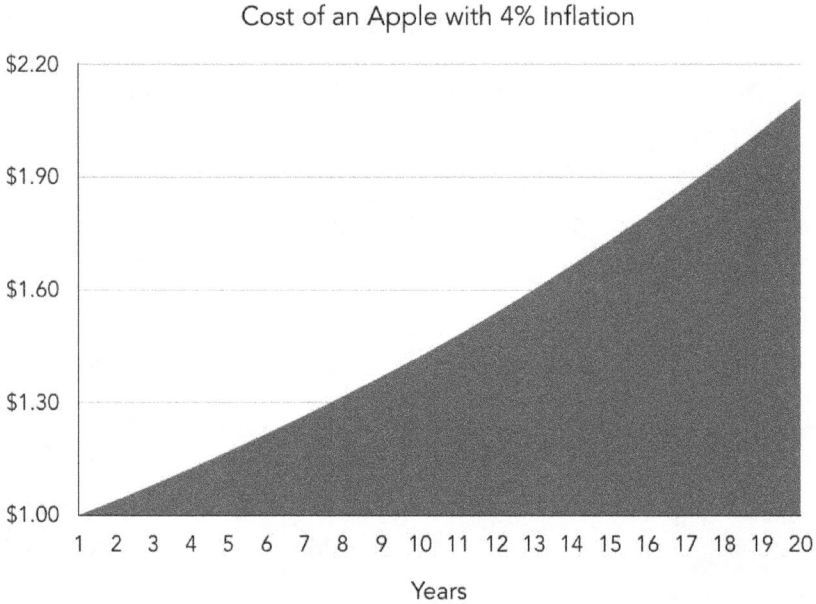

Understanding the effect of inflation means you need to put your money to work so it grows faster than the inflation rate. Leaving money sitting in a bank account earning an interest rate less than inflation means the *value* of your money is going down (even though the amount might be increasing).

— RICH HABIT —

The Rich know that inflation is the devaluation of money and put their money to work to beat inflation.

— POOR HABIT —

The Poor are oblivious to and victimized by inflation.

There is, however, another effect that inflation has that is often overlooked: the effect it has on the amount of tax you pay.

Inflation and Tax

In most developed countries around the world today we have an increasing tax rate. The more money you earn, the higher the percentage of tax is taken from your income. Inflation increases the cost in living, which puts pressure on employers to pay more money because people need more money to live. Higher income results in an increase in the percentage of tax paid. The end result, despite earning more money (because more is needed to live), your buying power is reduced due to paying more tax!

Here's a diagram that helps explain this.

Effect of Inflation

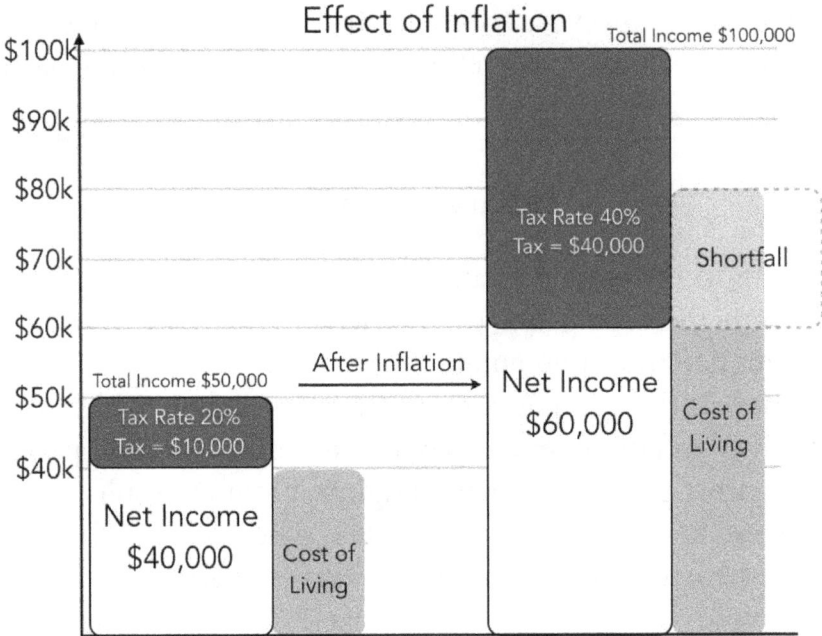

In the example above, inflation has halved the value of the money, which has doubled the cost of living. This doesn't happen overnight of course, but over many years; however, this example is used to highlight the point that inflation, while it devalues your money, increases your tax rate.

The result: Although income has also doubled to match inflation, it is now taxed at a higher rate. Therefore, the net income has only increased by 50% from $40,000 to $60,000 while the cost of living has doubled to $80,000 resulting in a shortfall.

Net Income & Cost of Living at 4% Inflation

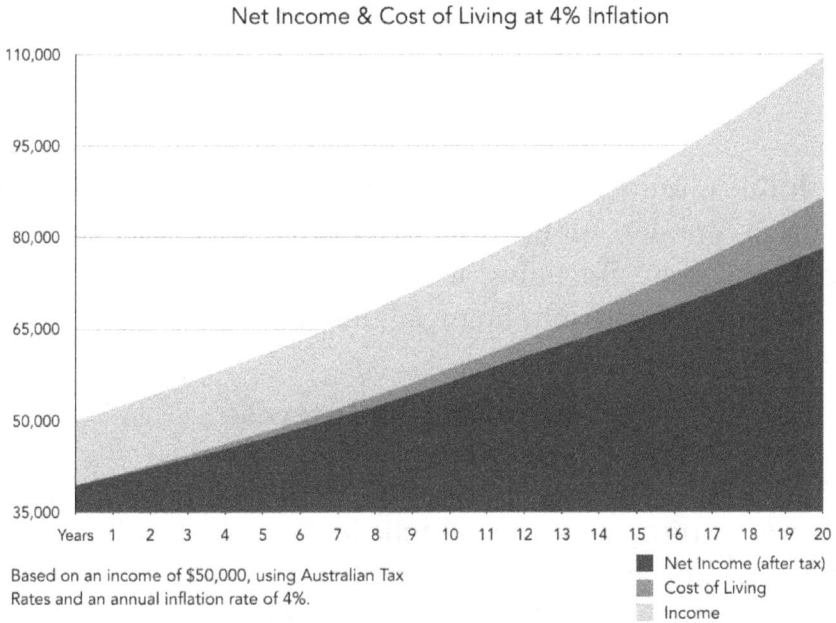

Based on an income of $50,000, using Australian Tax
Rates and an annual inflation rate of 4%.

■ Net Income (after tax)
▨ Cost of Living
▨ Income

The above graph shows the cost of living rising above the net income. Initially, the cost of living is equal to their net income of $40,000 (they spend all they make). Both the income and cost of living are increasing at 4% per year. But because of the increasing tax rate, the net income falls below the cost of living. The Australian tax rates of July 2008 are used in this example. It's an interesting exercise to compare your current buying power to that of 10 or 20 years ago. The result may not be as drastic as in the example above, but just because you earn more today doesn't mean you have more buying power.

— RICH HABIT —

The Rich know inflation acts like a hidden tax.

The Poor are unknowingly taxed more because of inflation.

If this is quite a shock to you, then realize this: You now have a greater motivation to control your money and make it grow. Spending it unwisely and not investing is what leads people into financial difficulty.

Compounding Interest

Another aspect of money is how it can grow. Understanding money includes understanding the phenomenon of compounding interest. *Compounding* means adding to the original amount, making it larger.

Compounding interest is the act of reinvesting your returns. For example, if you invest $10.00 and generate a 10% return, you make $1.00; now you have $11.00. If you make another 10%, you make $1.10, and suddenly, your profits are getting bigger, even though you're still making a 10% return.

It's like folding a piece of paper in half: the more you fold it, the thicker it gets. Each fold makes it twice as thick as before. This is the effect of compounding interest and, in the finance sense, it is money making money!

$10 Growing at 10%

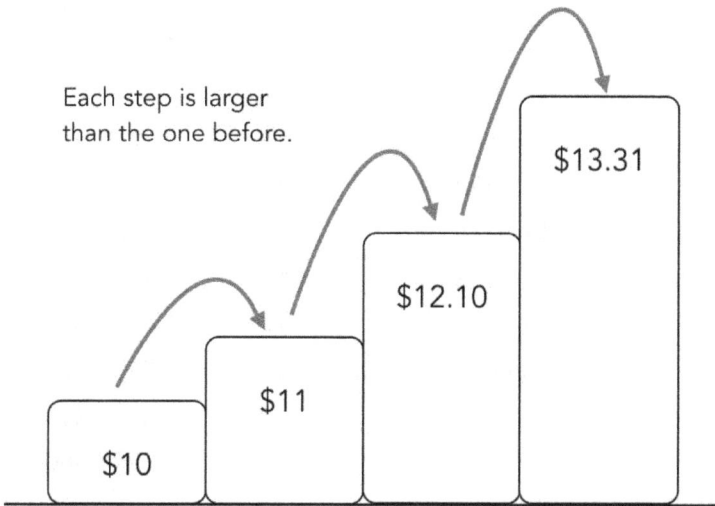

Each step is larger
than the one before.

$13.31

$12.10

$11

$10

If you started with $10,000 and invested it at 20% return per year, in five years, you would have $24,883; in ten years, you'd have $61,971, and in twenty years, you'd have $383,376, as shown in the table below.

$10,000 Invested at 20% Return Per Year

Year	Amount	Year	Amount
Start	$10,000		
1	$12,000	11	$74,301
2	$14,400	12	$89,161
3	$17,280	13	$106,993
4	$20,736	14	$128,392
5	$24,883	15	$154,070
6	$29,860	16	$184,884
7	$35,832	17	$221,861
8	$42,998	18	$266,233
9	$51,598	19	$319,480
10	$61,917	20	$383,376

$10,000 Invested at 20% Return Per Year

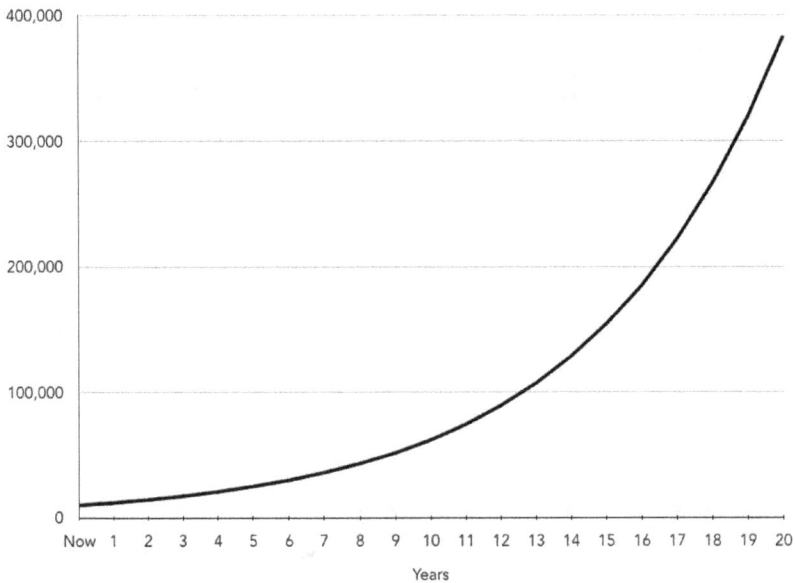

Compounding interest is great for the investor when accumulating wealth. But the same principle applies in the opposite direction. If you have debt, the interest on the debt (if left unpaid) creates a compounding effect, creating more debt. While a compounding interest graph for investments goes up, a graph of compounding interest on debt goes down. For example, any debt on a credit card at 20% interest would more than double in 4 years time if nothing was paid towards the debt.

It's easy to see from the following graph that fighting compounding interest takes extra effort. It's much better to have compounding interest working for you, as an investor, than having it working against you. Here's the Rich Habit that applies:

— RICH HABIT —

The Rich utilize the effect of compounding interest to boost their wealth.

— POOR HABIT —

The Poor get trapped into never-ending debt because of compounding interest.

$10,000 Debt 20% Interest

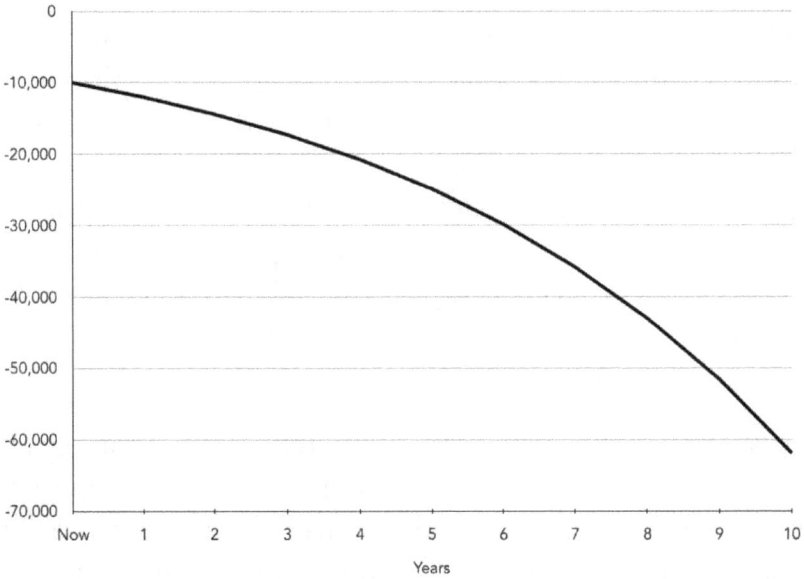

With these vital Rich Habits under your belt, let's take a look at what it is you are truly trying to achieve financially.

5

YOUR TWO MAIN GOALS

I have found there is quite a bit of confusion about what people should focus on: Some say that cash flow is king and encourage people to earn more income. Others say building assets is the key because that builds true wealth. And there are some who believe that debt is bad and you should never get into debt. These different beliefs all have valid points, but they have failed to clarify the overall financial goal that *everybody* should be aiming for.

Your goal is increasing **solvency**. The definition of the word "solvent" is *having more assets than debt*, it means being able to pay one's debts and bills in full. It comes from the Latin word *solvere,* which means *dissolve*. In essence, if you are solvent, your wealth can dissolve *all* your debt.

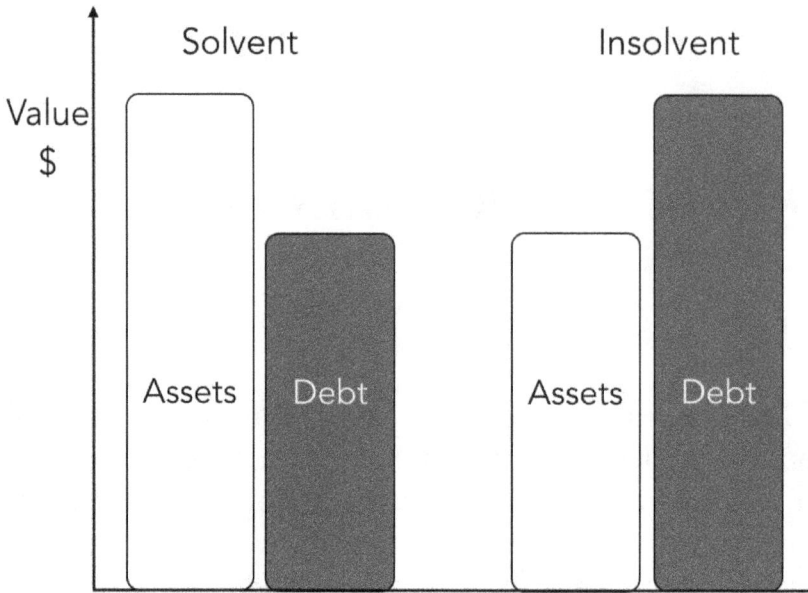

As mentioned earlier, you must have a positive goal to focus on. "Being debt-free" is not a goal. We want to have a goal that provides direction. To get away from something does not provide any clear direction or target. A clearly defined goal provides direction and focus. Hence, solvency is the first goal.

Solvency can be positive or negative. When it is negative, we call it insolvency.

There are different degrees of insolvency; a person can be a little insolvent or very insolvent, as illustrated below.

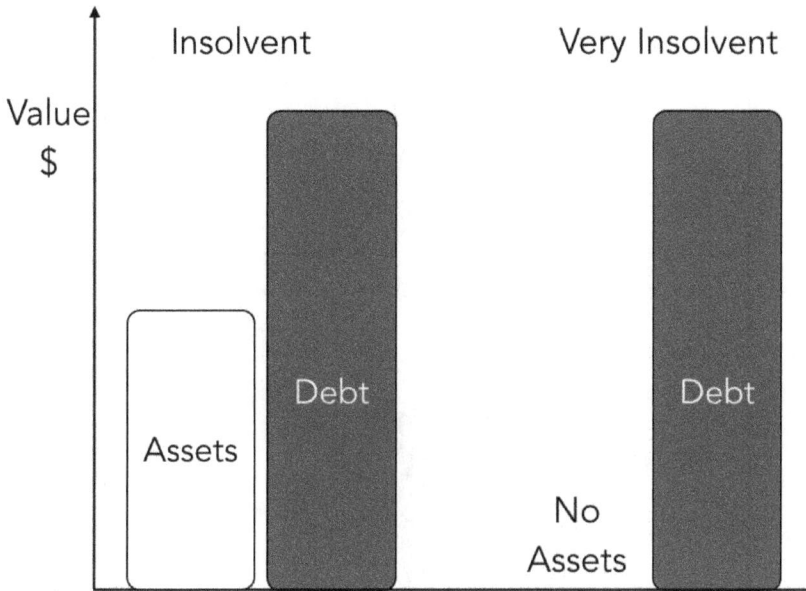

No matter how insolvent you are, you can get back to zero and become solvent.

— RICH HABITS FORMULA —

Solvency = value of assets less total debt.

Solvency Forumla

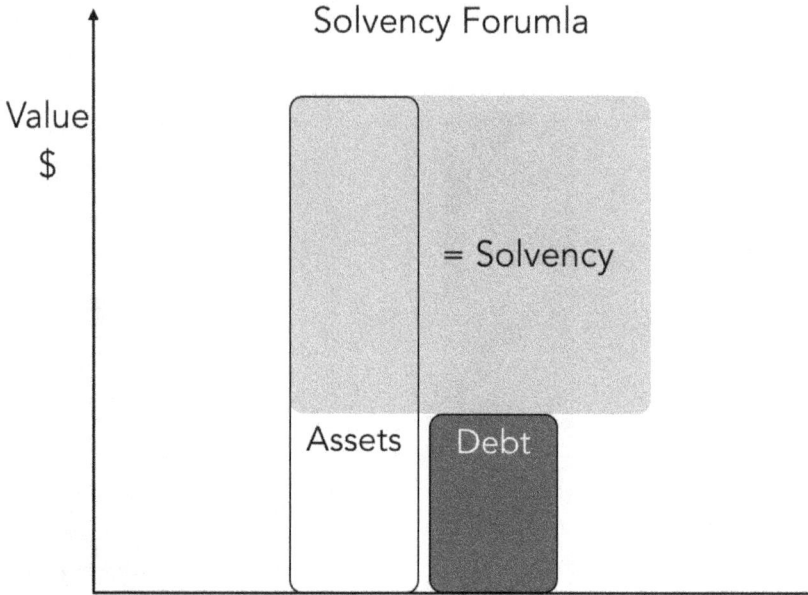

You are aiming for a constantly increasing solvency. This does not mean having no debt, by the way. Debt against valuable assets, such as property, is good debt as long as the asset increases in value.

Here's an example that highlights this point:

Both Ben and Dave are Solvent

Value
$

Assets

Debt

Assets

No
Debt

Ben

Dave

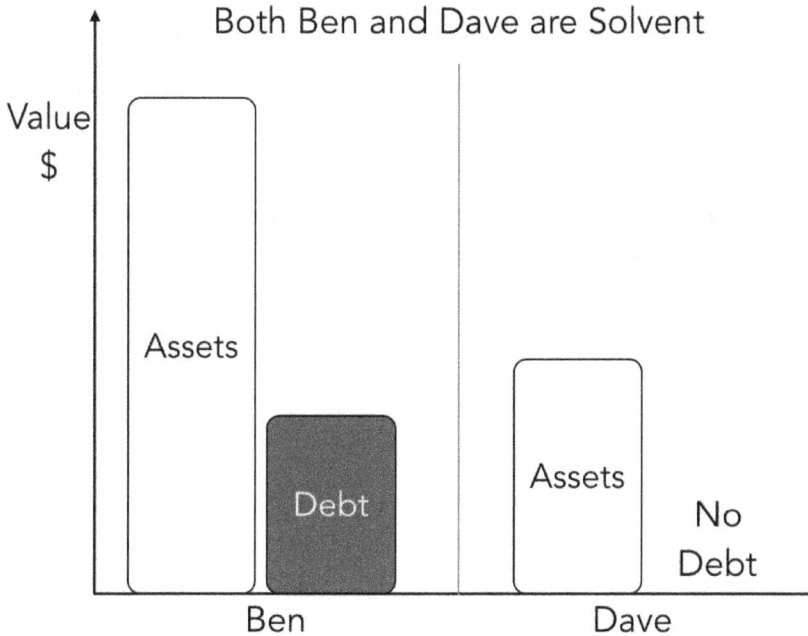

In the example above, both Ben and Dave are solvent even though Ben has debt. In fact, Ben is more solvent than Dave. The above graph is represented in numbers in the table below to demonstrate that Ben is worth more than Dave, even though Dave has no debt.

Name	Ben	Dave
Total Asset Value	500,000	200,000
Less Total Debt	-100,000	0
Solvency	**400,000**	**200,000**

If Ben sold his assets, he would have more money than Dave. Also, if Ben's assets are such things as property and shares (assets that usually increase in value over time), Ben will become much wealthier than Dave in the long run because he has a larger asset base to begin with. This is why "no debt" is not our goal; our goal is increasing solvency, which is one of the fundamental Rich Habits.

— RICH HABIT —

The Rich are solvent and constantly improve it.

— POOR HABIT —

The Poor tolerate being insolvent.

Your Second Goal

Your second goal is to be viable. Being viable means *your income is greater than your expenses.* The word "viable" means *capable of living and growing*; it comes from the Latin word *vita* which means *life!* If you are viable you can live and grow. If you are not viable, you are spending more than you make and will soon not be able to live very well at all. Here's the formula for viability:

— RICH HABITS FORMULA —

Viability = income is greater than or equal to your expenses.

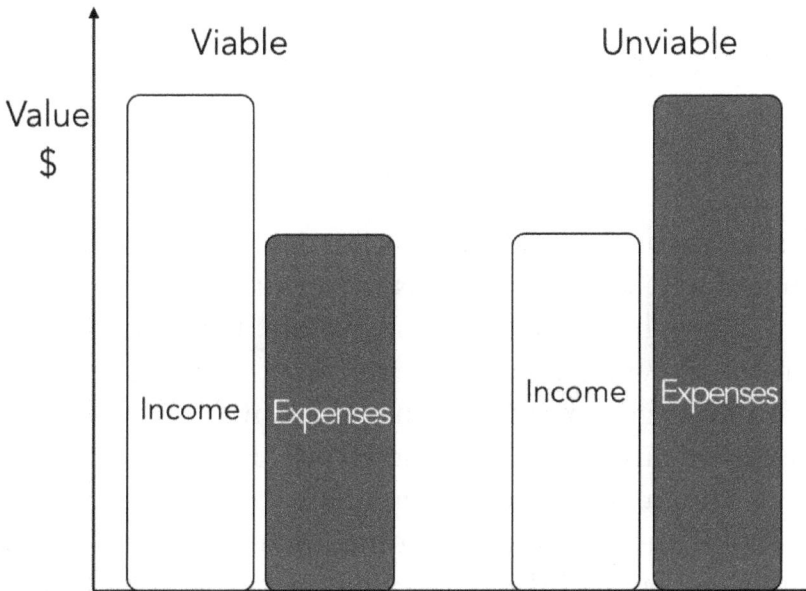

This provides us with another fundamental Rich Habit:

— RICH HABIT —

The Rich are always viable.

— POOR HABIT —

The Poor tolerate being unviable.

Understanding these fundamental Rich Habits provides us with simple definitions for "Rich" and "Poor."

— RICH HABITS DEFINITIONS —

Rich is being abundantly solvent and viable.

Poor is being insolvent and unviable.

Truly Rich

Using these definitions, we can easily identify who is Rich and who isn't. Just because a person owns a fancy car and a fancy house doesn't make them Rich, if they are insolvent, they are Poor. A person with an average house and an average car is far Richer than most. That is why, throughout this book, I use the terms "Rich" and "Poor" with a capital letter, to differentiate between the usual definitions and ideas surrounding these concepts. When we talk of being "Rich," we mean being solvent and viable. And it is much easier for a person with an average house, earning an average income to be Rich than it is for those who are burdened with overwhelming debt, living in a fancy house. The amount of money has nothing to do it, solvency and viability are your only yardstick.

Measuring Your Solvency & Viability

Now that you understand the two main goals, you must measure them to see if they are improving or getting worse. There's an old business saying: *"You can't manage what you don't measure."* This is never more truer than with your finances.

If you want to manage your money and become solvent, you must measure your finances constantly.

The best way to measure and monitor your solvency and viability is to graph them on a regular basis. If you get paid weekly, graph them weekly. If it's monthly, do it monthly.

Regardless of how often you get paid, you should monitor them at least every month.

Let's take a look at an example of a solvency graph.

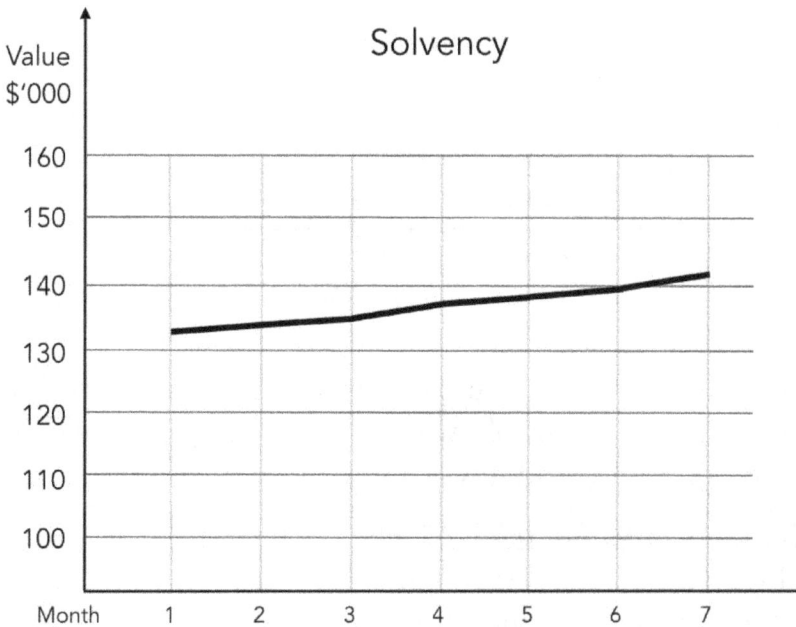

Remember, this figure is the difference between your assets and debt. The graph above shows a positive solvency, growing slightly every month. If it is not positive, it means you are insolvent and your graph may look like this:

Negative Solvency (Insolvency)

Value $'000

10

Zero

-10

-20

-30

-40

-50

Month   1   2   3   4   5   6   7

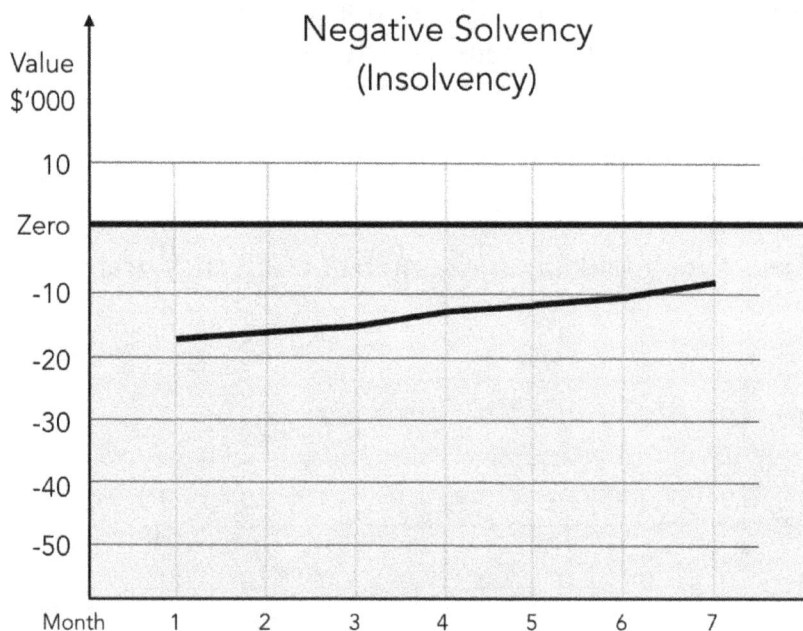

By the way, if you are insolvent, don't be too disheartened; my graph was negative $300,000 when I started doing this, and it was going down!

It's at this point that I'd like to introduce to you an analogy that we'll use throughout the rest of this book. I'm sure you've heard of the phrase "keeping your head above water." It means you are managing to survive financially, but only just.

When insolvent, think of yourself as a swimmer. Zero solvency is at water level. When insolvent, you are underwater. When solvent, you are above water.

Solvency Graph

Solvency $

Positive

Zero

Negative

Water Level
(Zero Solvency)

Above Water (solvent)

Solvency

Underwater (insolvent)

Month 1   2   3   4   5   6   7

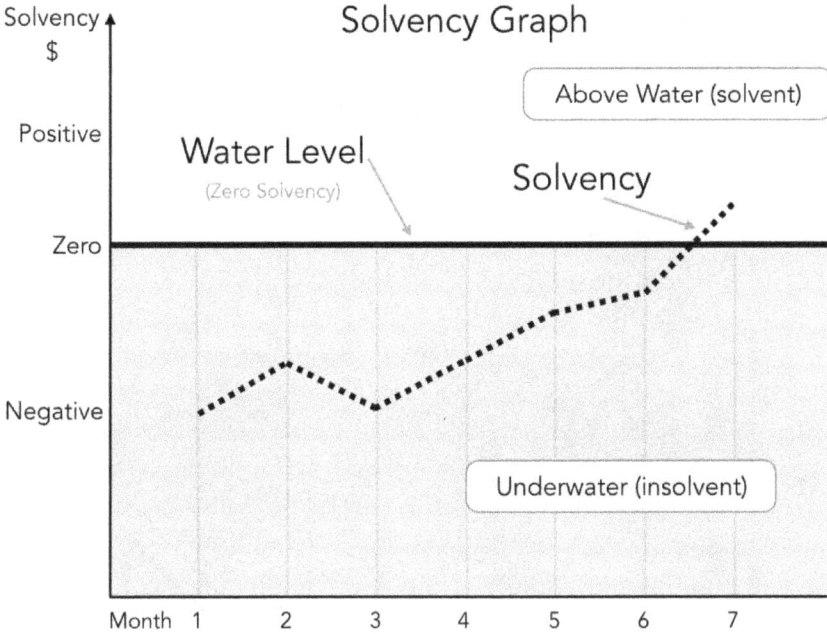

When you improve your solvency, you are swimming towards the surface, and when solvency decreases you start sinking. I can't over-stress how important it is to graph this. If you are very insolvent, like I was, it's important to keep track of this because it will make you feel better when you see you're swimming in the right direction!

Of course, our goal is not to just get our heads above water, we want an increasing solvency that goes way above zero! So, what happens when you get to zero and above water level? Ever heard of the term "high-flyer?" That's someone who is doing very well financially. When you move above zero, that is when you really take off!

The whole essence of this book is to give you "Financial Wings" to help you fly.

So that is how you measure your solvency. Now let's

take a look at how you measure your viability.

Measuring Viability

Viability is having an income greater than your living expenses. It is best graphed as a comparison of your income and expenses.

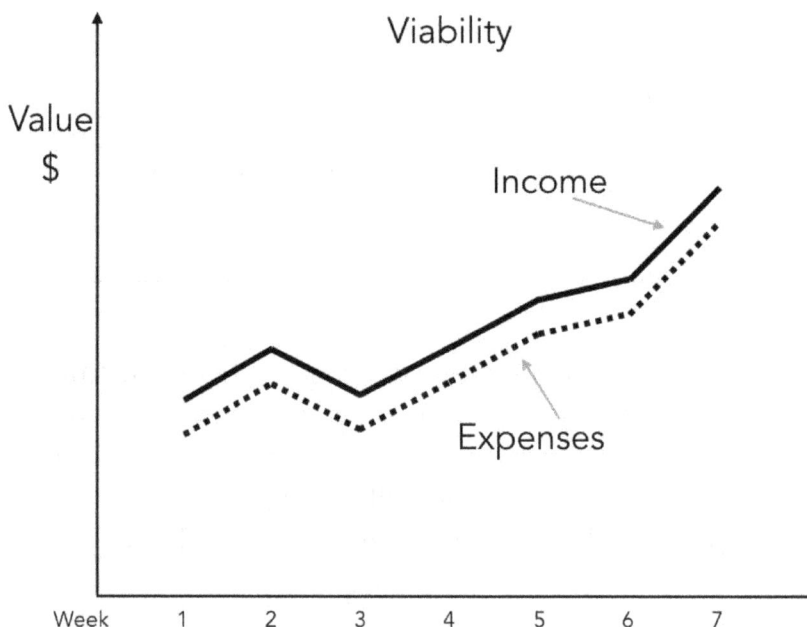

When the income line is above the expenses line, you are viable. The bigger the gap between your income and expenses the more viable you are.

If someone spends more than they make, their graph looks like this:

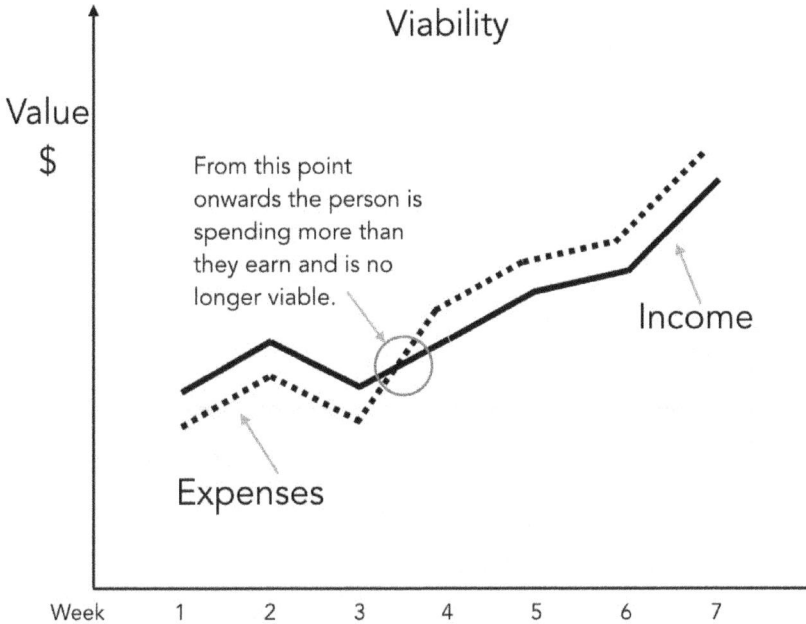

Viability

Value
$

From this point
onwards the person is
spending more than
they earn and is no
longer viable.

Income

Expenses

Week   1   2   3   4   5   6   7

In the example above, from weeks 4 to 7 this person was spending more than they made—we call this unviable. Unviable, as you may have guess is the opposite of being viable, it means *the person is unable to live,* they are borrowing money each week, (using credit cards for example) which also means they became more insolvent because their debt increased.

This tells us something about viability—*it affects your solvency.* To help you grasp this concept, let's extend our swimming analogy: When insolvent viability shows which *direction* you are *swimming.* If you are viable and spending less than you make then you are swimming *upwards,* if you are spending everything that you make then you are swimming *sideways* and finally, if you are unviable you are swimming *deeper.*

Of course, if you are solvent then your viability indicates

which *direction* you are *flying* and whether you need to put on a lifejacket!

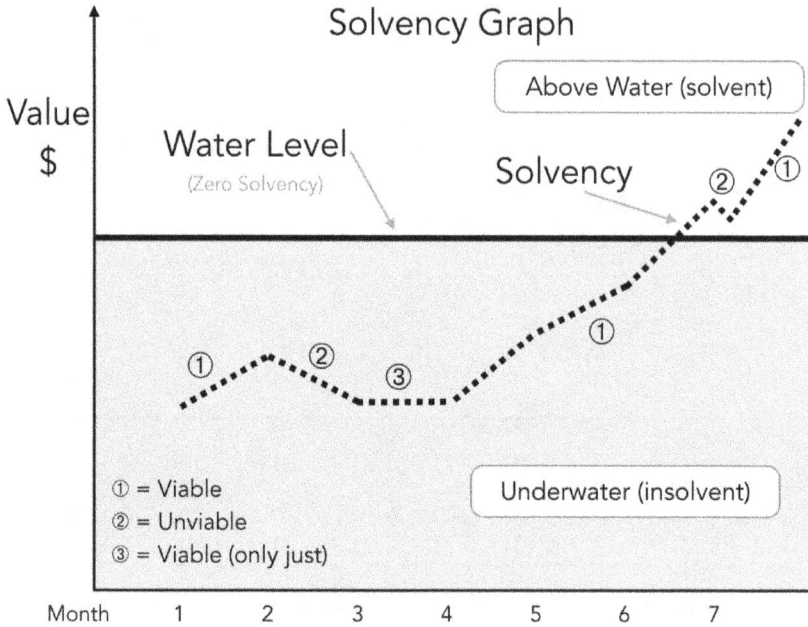

Solvency Graph

Value
$

Water Level
(Zero Solvency)

Above Water (solvent)

Solvency

② ①

① = Viable
② = Unviable
③ = Viable (only just)

Underwater (insolvent)

Month   1   2   3   4   5   6   7

You can see how your solvency and viability affect each other. They are interconnected. Viability gives you life and helps you get your head above water. As you'll discover in the coming chapters, managing your viability is how you grow financial wings.

Slowly Drowning

The concepts of solvency and viability provide an insight into why big companies "suddenly" go broke despite earning millions of dollars.

In reality, such companies have been slowly swimming deeper. Perhaps financial records have been manipulated to "look good." Some debt can be left out of the equations and asset values can be inflated. The end result of this "creative accounting" is a slowly drowning company.

This is not just bad financial management, it's dishonest.

If you want to drown slowly then falsify the numbers. If you want to be solvent, be honest about the numbers. After all, the math is not that hard is it? I think a child could follow the equation of Asset Values minus Debt and get it right as long the numbers are accurate.

Any organization and any individual can prevent financial disaster by just knowing their solvency and viability. Putting both on a graph shows immediately whether things are getting better or worse. And if they are getting worse don't change the numbers to fix it, fix it for real! That's where honesty comes in.

Accurate numbers and the guts to face the *real* situation is all it takes to be in control of your finances. It's not rocket science. The fact that it's not done comes down to the lack of education in this area and the courage and honesty of those in control of money: To do otherwise is to practice Poor Habits.

Relationship Between Solvency & Viability

As mentioned, solvency and viability both affect each other. There are many situations an individual or company can find themselves in. Let's explore these to help you understand the relationship between solvency and viability, and gain an insight into your own situation.

Take a look at the following graphs.

Scenario One - Kim

Solvency

Viability

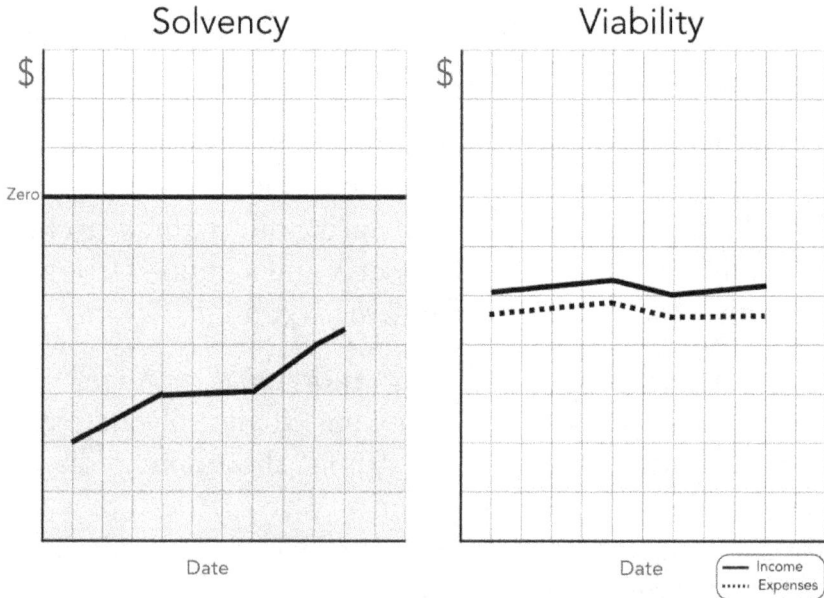

The Solvency Graph shows that Kim is insolvent. The reason for her insolvency could have been bad investment decisions, possible business failure or simply poor spending habits using credit cards and store cards. How Kim got into this situation is irrelevant at this stage. Kim now knows she has to swim upwards to get solvent again. We can see from Kim's Viability Graph that she is spending less than she makes. Both graphs are heading in the right direction. If Kim continues with her good control of money and develops Rich Habits, she will achieve solvency and create true wealth.

Scenario Two - Karl

Solvency

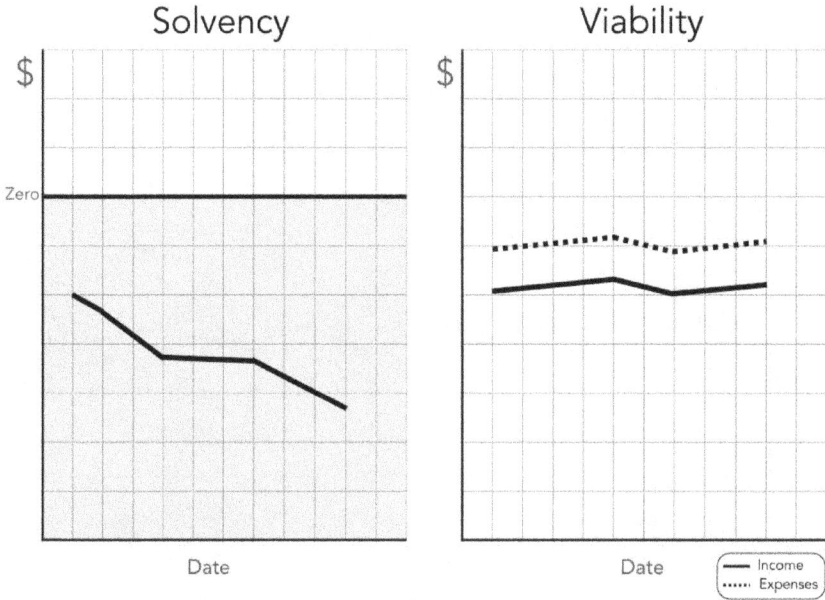

Viability

Karl is in trouble! Not only is he insolvent but he's also unviable; he continues to spend more than he is making, which in turn, makes him more insolvent. Karl is swimming downwards and from the look of these graphs, you can tell that Karl is not keeping up with his debt repayments, further increasing his debt, dragging him deeper. The first step Karl must do is to get viable immediately: cut expenses back straight away and increase his income in some way. This situation cannot be continued any longer and needs to be fixed ASAP. (I will explain how to get out of this situation in the coming chapters.)

Scenario Three - Kath

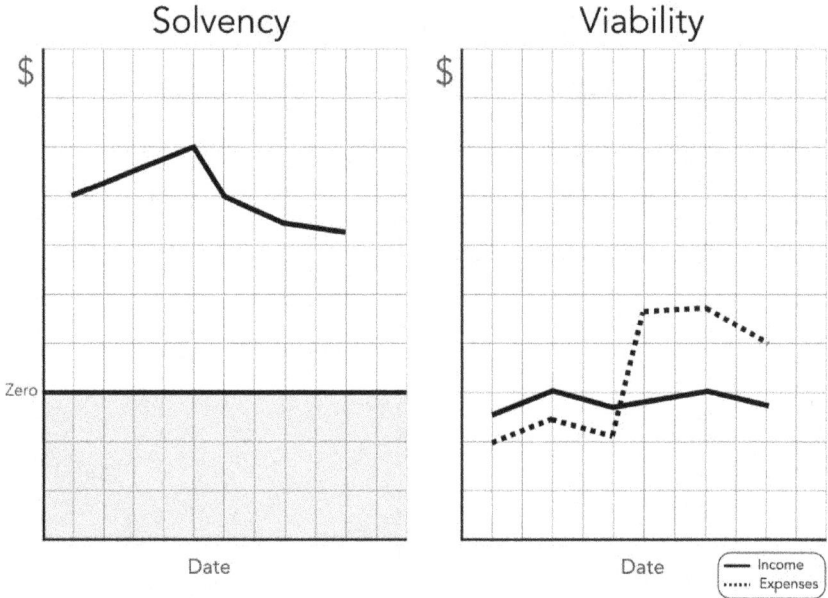

Kath definitely has an issue here, but it's not as bad as Karl's situation. Although she is unviable, she is solvent. Many people find themselves in this scenario: asset-rich but cash-flow poor. This situation occurs when there is an unexpected rise in interest rates, for example, which is possibly what has happened to Kath. When bills or mortgage payments can't be paid, the usual solution for most people is to sell an asset to pay down the debt. But the problem is not with solvency—it's with viability. A better solution, for the long term, is to reduce other expenses without selling any assets, while finding ways to increase income; this approach would improve viability and resolve the problem.

This kind of graph is common for people or companies who have long gaps between income. An example of this is in property development. I've been in the situation of being owed a lot of money but had to wait until the property was completed before receiving full payment. The same applies to sales commissions and other types of sporadic income industries. The key to surviving this scenario is to have tight financial control and a good relationship with your creditors or suppliers. When the big money comes in, you must allocate it sensibly for future expenses.

Therefore, if Kath can get viable, she doesn't need to sell her assets. With tight financial control, she could keep soaring higher and higher.

Scenario Four - Kane

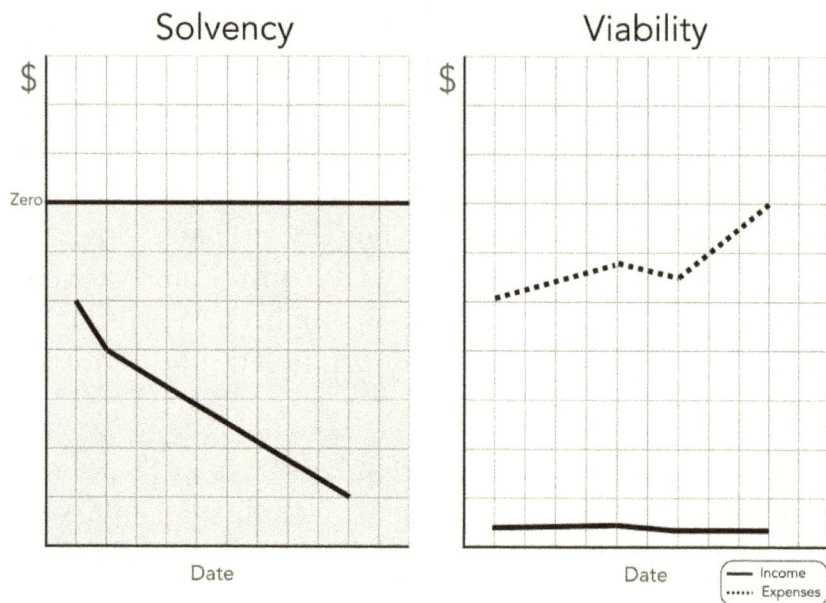

Solvency

Viability

Uh oh, this is bad! Kane is in deep water and moments away from bankruptcy. Kane needs to read this book quickly and get into action! It starts with getting viable, increasing income and writing letters to all his creditors. Despite such a dismal picture, it is possible to recover even from this—I know because these were my graphs! The reason Kane got into this situation was because he never knew his solvency or viability and never graphed them. He might have sensed things weren't going well, but his failure to really face the situation was his real downfall. Kane would have had a graph like Karl in Scenario Two many months ago. But now that Kane knows his situation, he can at least start the long journey upwards and start swimming like mad to the surface before the sharks get him. It's not a pleasant situation but when he hits the surface, which he will if he knows and follows the Rich Habits, the euphoria he'll feel cannot be expressed in words. Trust me!

I hope that by covering these scenarios, you can see how both your solvency and viability are vital to know and monitor. It should be apparent that unviability is the first step towards insolvency. On the flip side, viability is also the first step towards improving solvency. Maintaining viability is the key to solvency and long-term prosperity. Being unviable is never tolerated by the Rich; only the Poor tolerate being unviable.

Unviability and the accumulation of the wrong type of debt creates insolvency. To control money and follow the Rich Habits, you must understand the true purpose of debt.

6

THE TRUE PURPOSE OF DEBT

△

The reason debt is considered by so many to be a bad thing lies in the fact that it is often used for the wrong purpose. There are two types of debt: good debt and bad debt. Unfortunately, the English language doesn't provide a different word for these two types of debt, so "debt" in general gets a bad name.

To easily differentiate between the two types of debt, good debt should be called "investment debt" because debt against investments that increase in value, increase your solvency.

Debt that is used to buy things that have little or no value (like TVs or holidays) is "bad debt." It is sad that people get caught up in this cycle of never-ending debt. Some refer to bad debt as "consumer debt," but a better name for it, one that would help people avoid it, is "killer debt." It is a rock that weighs you down, much like it would weigh a swimmer down. The cruelest thing you could do to someone treading water, or someone who was having difficulty keeping their head above water, would be to hand them a big heavy rock! Now they have to work twice as hard to keep afloat or as is too often the case, simply start to sink. Killer debt does that to those who are barely solvent. It makes them sink.

The true purpose of debt is to buy investments; use it to buy anything else and you are swimming in the wrong direction.

Investments are like rockets that lift you to higher heights. Investment debt is the rocket fuel that speeds up your progress.

Investment debt is a tool used to buy more investments. Killer debt, on the other hand, should be gotten rid of fast because it is nothing but a burden.

To be very clear, here's the definition of the two types of debt:

— RICH HABITS DEFINITION —

Investment debt is money borrowed to buy assets that increase in value and/or provide an income.

Killer debt is money owed that is not backed by assets. It includes overdue or unpaid bills.

It's the combination of killer debt and spending more than one makes that has given debt a bad name. The truth of the matter is that insolvency is what is bad—it should have a bad name, not "debt." Without the ability to borrow money to invest or start a business, it would be very difficult for the average income earner to build wealth. Investment debt speeds up the process of wealth creation when following the Rich Habits.

— RICH HABIT —

The Rich use debt to invest (Investment debt).

— POOR HABIT —

The Poor use debt to spend (Killer debt).

Three Types of Investments

While I've devoted a whole chapter to the subject of investing, it's important that you have a basic understanding of the types of investment categories before we cover how to control money.

These 3 categories are:

1. Direct Investments

2. Business

3. Education in Yourself

Direct Investments

Direct investments include anything that increases in value over time and may also provide an income, such as property and shares. Antiques and jewelry are assets; although they don't produce an income, they can increase in value. Borrowing money to buy direct investments is the most popular method used to build wealth.

Business

You can invest in your own business or one run by

another. If run correctly, a business is something that can rapidly increase in value. Debt used to buy, start or expand a business can produce an increase in income and in the value of the business, improving both your solvency and viability.

Education in Yourself

This is the most important investment you can make, and you'll find it to be the most lucrative. An individual can increase their earning potential by learning more about their profession. A business owner can increase the profits and value of their business by learning more about "business," such as: marketing, promotion, staff recruitment and management. Everyone should also invest in their own financial education, whether employee or business owner. No matter how you make money, you need to know where to put it so it grows (and beats inflation). Understanding how to invest your money in shares or property provides you with the knowledge to increase your solvency while earning money doing what you enjoy.

Investment Lag

The investments methods mentioned above often suffer from a lag between investing the money and receiving a return. The more you learn, the smaller this lag can be and the greater the profits. The more experienced you become at investing, the less chance you have of losing money.

Investment Lag

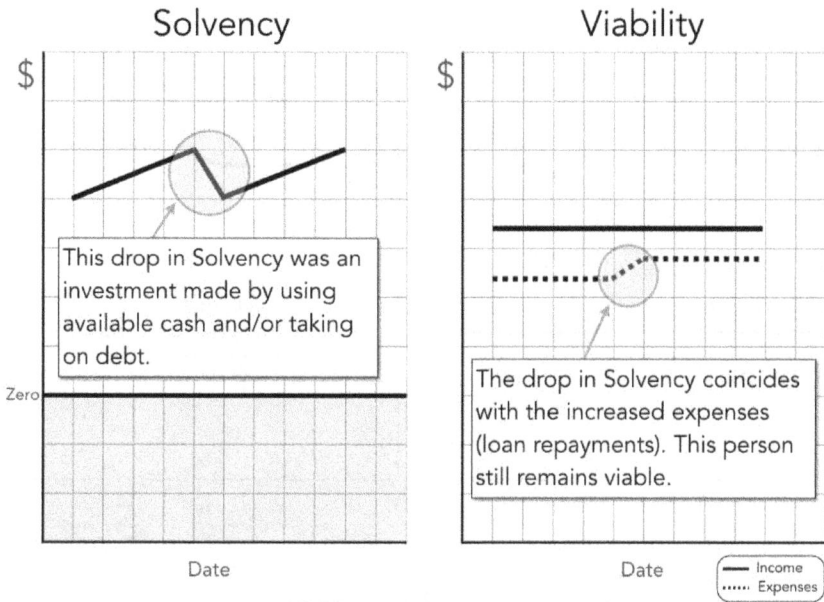

Solvency

This drop in Solvency was an investment made by using available cash and/or taking on debt.

Viability

The drop in Solvency coincides with the increased expenses (loan repayments). This person still remains viable.

Following are several scenarios of how the investment above will eventually play out.

Property Investment

Let's assume the above investment was a property you purchased to rent out to tenants. Before renting it out, you organize some minor repairs and renovations. Once the tenant moves in, you start receiving additional income from the rent. After several months, you have the property revalued and it has increased. The following graph illustrates the change in solvency and viability.

Investment Lag - Property Investment

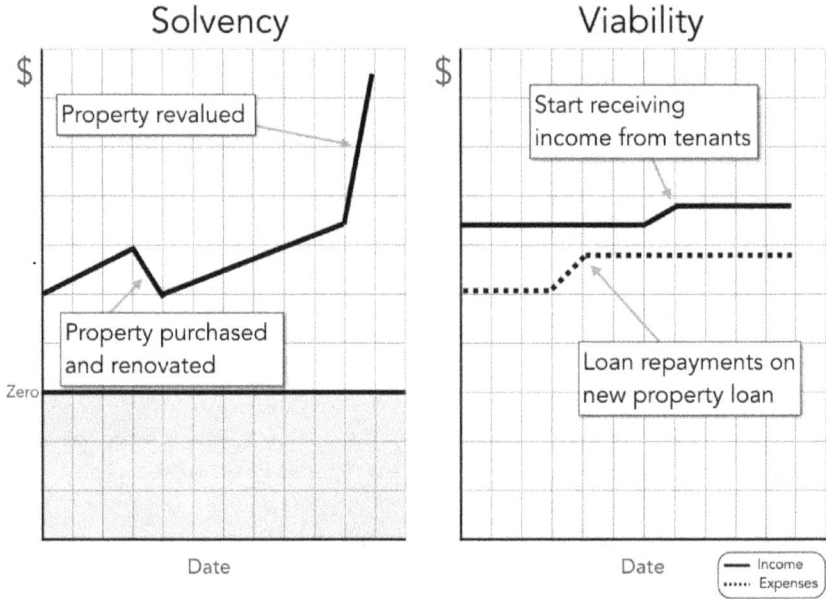

Solvency

Property revalued

Property purchased and renovated

Zero

Date

Viability

Start receiving income from tenants

Loan repayments on new property loan

Date

Income ——
Expenses ······

Education Investment

For this scenario let's assume you have invested in a share trading course, where you learned a proven strategy on how to choose undervalued companies that are likely to grow over the next 6 months. You use a credit card to pay for the cost of the course, and this reduces your solvency.

Investment Lag - Education Investment

Solvency

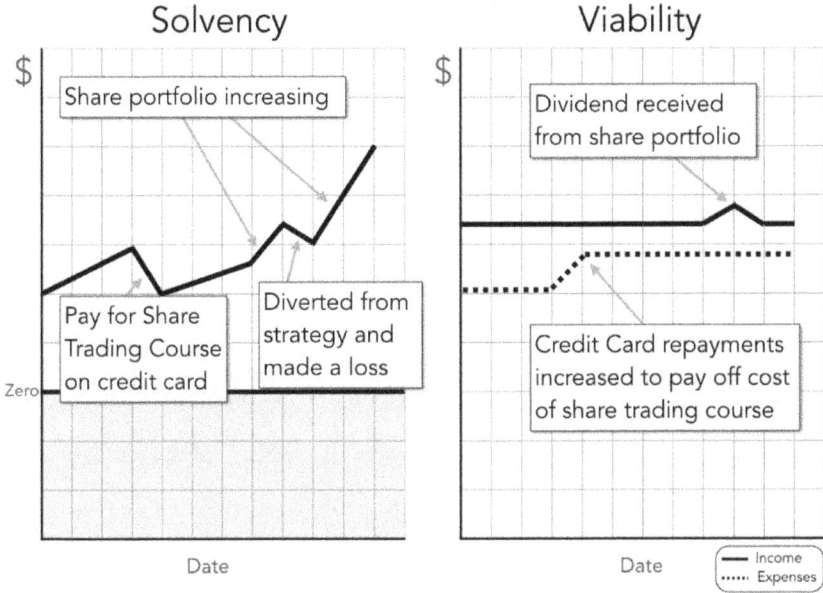

$

Share portfolio increasing

Pay for Share Trading Course on credit card

Diverted from strategy and made a loss

Zero

Date

Viability

$

Dividend received from share portfolio

Credit Card repayments increased to pay off cost of share trading course

Date

—— Income
······ Expenses

Shortly after attending the course, you immediately apply what you have learned and choose several companies that are undervalued, per the criteria. After a few months, your share portfolio has increased and with your added confidence, you start to look for more investing opportunities. You decide to invest in a company that doesn't fit the criteria you were taught, but you've got a hunch so you go for it. Within the month, you wipe out almost half your previous gains and decide to stick to the strategy. Fortunately, a surprise check comes in the mail to cheer you up: one of the companies you initially selected paid a dividend to shareholders. As your initial shares continue to rise, so does your solvency—now you're starting to fly.

For some, the idea of taking on debt to fund their education appears rather risky. But using debt to pay for holidays and cars is a lot riskier than borrowing for education, because a holiday or car have decreasing or little value, whereas education when applied has unlimited value.

Take a look at these graphs, with the following numbers:

Solvency = zero; Income = zero; Expense = zero

Zero Graphs

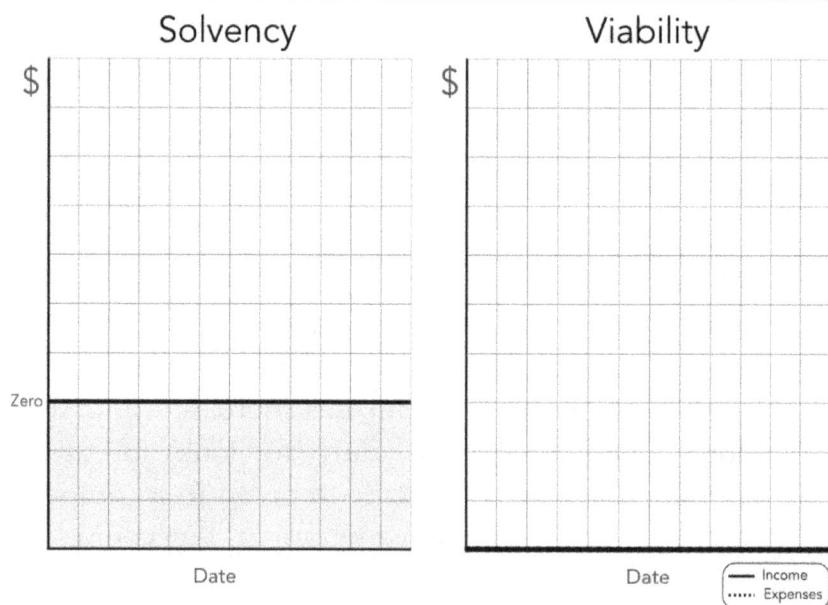

What can you tell from such graphs?

This person is either very young or not alive!

The point that I'm trying to make is that YOU are your most valuable asset. Your solvency and viability are not very important to you as a baby or when you are dead.

So, the best investment you can make is in you, because *only you* can increase the lines on the graph. And you can only do that through knowledge and application of that knowledge. Never be afraid to invest in yourself. And never be afraid to lose money on yourself either, because when you lose money, you've just made an investment in yourself and you learned something: what not to do!

Therefore the success of direct investments and business investments are dependent upon your education and experience. Don't ever be afraid of borrowing money to improve your knowledge and ability. It is the greatest investment you can make. Your only failure would be to make such an investment and never apply what you learn.

These are the Rich Habits that apply:

— RICH HABITS —

The Rich know that education in yourself is the best investment you can make.

The Rich never stop learning.

— POOR HABITS —

The Poor rarely invest in themselves.

The Poor think they already know and cease to learn.

Killer Debt

The scenarios above give you an idea of how investment debt affects your solvency and viability. Let's take a quick look at the effect of killer debt.

While out at the shops one day, you see the latest

flatscreen TV. It's the biggest and the best, and it's on special! While looking at it, a salesman approaches you and asks what you think. You admit it's a great TV, but you don't have the money for it at the moment. He says, "That's okay, you can purchase it interest free with no money down, and if you take one today, I'll throw in a DVD player."

After a few "ums and errs," you decide "What the heck, I'll take it!"

You hold movie nights at your place and proudly show all your friends. Six months goes by and now you have to pay for it. You don't have the money to pay the debt in full, so you pay the minimum balance. After a few months, you are shocked to discover that you now owe more for the TV than what you paid for it, as your minimum payment is not enough to cover the 25% interest rate. In a panic, you quickly sell the TV for less than a third of what you paid because a newer model is out now, and it's bigger, better and cheaper.

Using debt to spend is a Poor Habit, and the picture looks like this:

Killer Debt

Solvency

Viability

$

$

Purchased
TV on credit

Increasing debt
on TV loan

Minimum payment on TV
loan takes you very close
to not being viable

Zero

Interest Free
loan period

Sold the TV but
are still insolvent

Date

Date

Income
Expenses

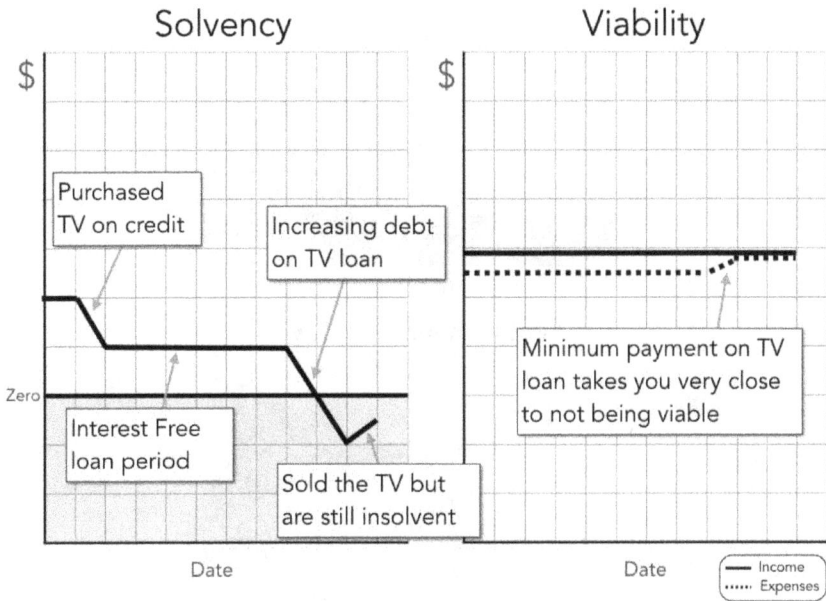

Reducing Your Investment Debt

Many people have the idea that they need to pay off their home mortgage as soon as possible. While this increases solvency, it is not necessarily the *fastest* way to do it.

As long as an investment is increasing in value greater than the interest rate on the loan, it is perfectly okay to pay the interest only, leaving the debt at the same level. The following graphs compare 1) paying interest only and 2) paying both the principal (which is the original amount of debt) and the interest. The interest-only graph shows the debt remaining the same, while the other graph shows the debt reducing because the principal is also being paid off.

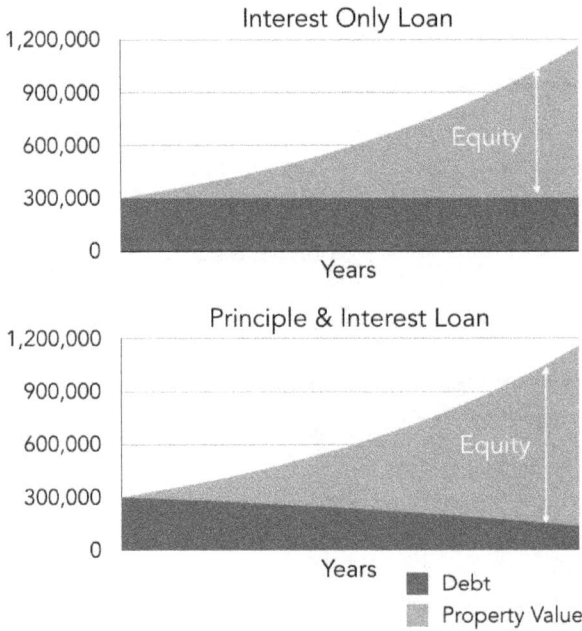

The difference between the property value and debt is called equity. As the equity increases so too does your solvency. Let's take a look at how these two methods affect your solvency and viability.

Rich Habits

Paying Interest Only

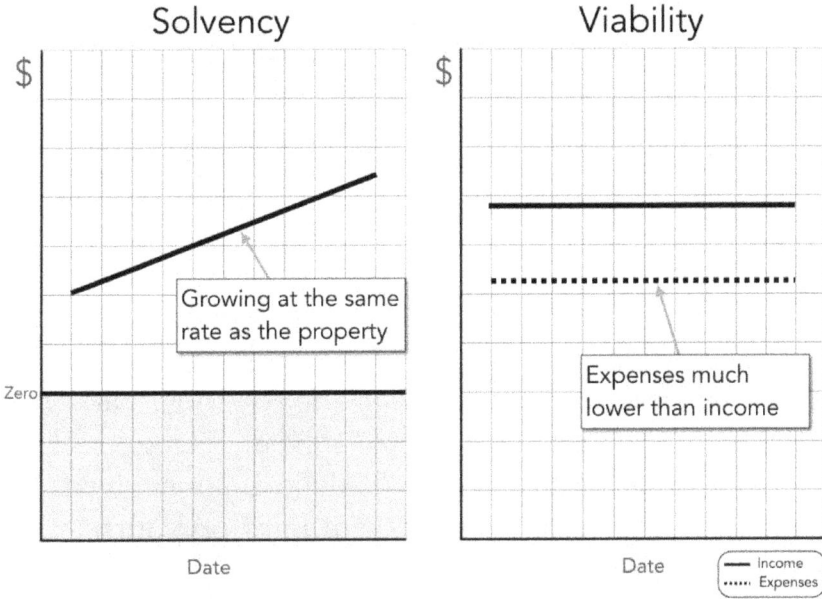

Solvency

$
Zero

Growing at the same rate as the property

Date

Viability

$

Expenses much lower than income

Date

— Income
...... Expenses

Paying Principal & Interest

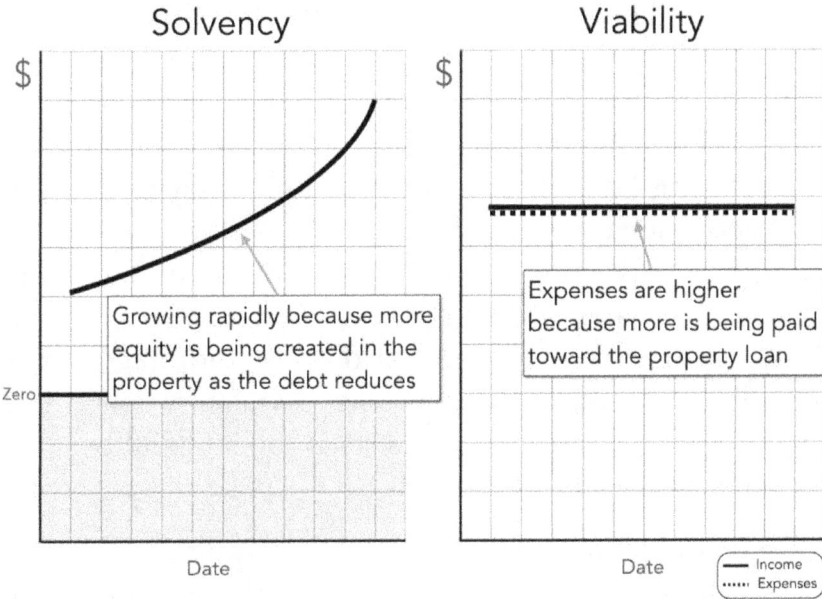

Solvency

$
Zero

Growing rapidly because more equity is being created in the property as the debt reduces

Date

Viability

$

Expenses are higher because more is being paid toward the property loan

Date

— Income
...... Expenses

Comparing these two loan payment methods, at first glance it appears that the better way to go is to reduce the debt as soon as possible—and this would be true, if the person was insolvent—but let's explore this more.

Your goal is increasing solvency. We know that being unviable is the first step toward insolvency. Therefore, it's vital that you maintain viability.

If a person was struggling to remain viable while paying principal and interest on their home loan, they could become viable by switching to an interest-only loan. The key point here is that, if you are solvent, being viable is more important than reducing the debt. If your solvency is positive and increasing, why make it hard on yourself and struggle to pay off the loan?

Another aspect to consider is the accumulation of more investments. The equity created in the first property can be used to buy more investments. If the person is only just viable (as in the principle and interest graph on the previous page), they would probably not even consider the idea of buying another property because, as far as they are concerned, they are only just surviving with one property. Buying an investment property would make them unviable. This is an all too common situation I see people fall into: in an endeavor to "get rid of the mortgage," they pour all their spare income into reducing debt. The thought of buying another property is too stressful because they believe they can't afford it.

Instead of looking at this from the viewpoint of "get out of debt," let's play the game of "increasing solvency" and focus on the positive goal instead of the negative goal.

Paying Interest Only

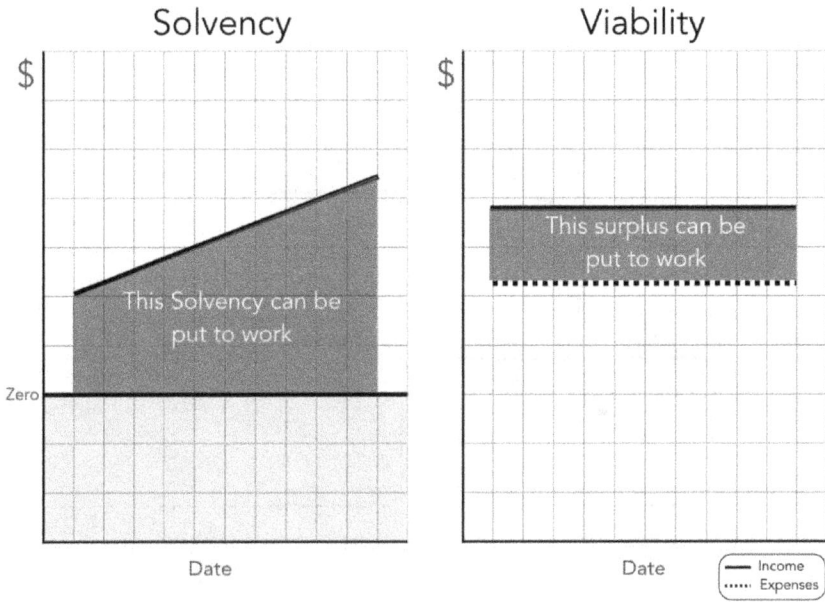

Solvency — This Solvency can be put to work

Viability — This surplus can be put to work

Income / Expenses

Your solvency can and should be put to work and so can the surplus of your viability.

When buying an investment, you know that it can temporarily reduce your solvency like the graphs below demonstrate.

Investor's Graph

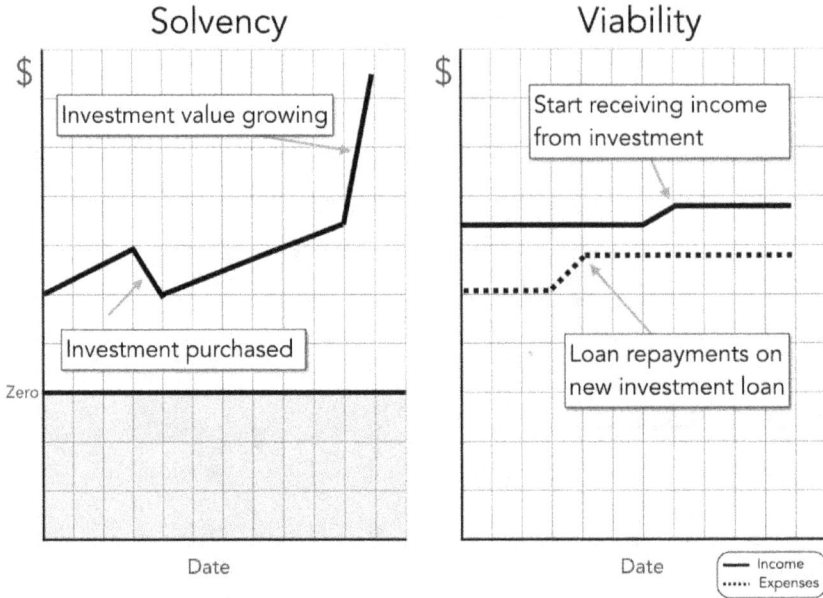

Solvency

$

Investment value growing

Investment purchased

Zero

Date

Viability

$

Start receiving income from investment

Loan repayments on new investment loan

Date

— Income
...... Expenses

Compare this to the "get-out-of-debt" focused graphs below.

Paying Principal & Interest

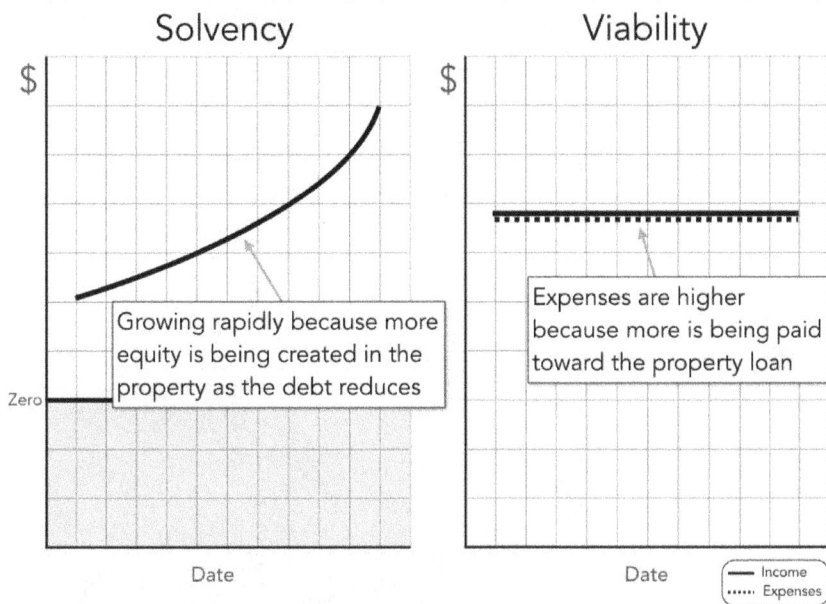

Solvency

Growing rapidly because more equity is being created in the property as the debt reduces

Viability

Expenses are higher because more is being paid toward the property loan

When comparing the illustration above with the prior investor's graph, at first glance, it appears the investor has made a mistake and gone to a lot more effort, with not much more reward, as far as their solvency goes. The thing to remember is that investing is a *time* game. The more you accumulate *today,* the more you'll have *tomorrow.* For example, if an investor has $1 million worth of assets increase in value by 10%, they have increased their solvency by $100,000. The person with an investment worth only $300,000 that increases at the same rate, has made only $30,000.

Take a look at the difference between starting with $300,000 worth of assets (your home for example) and

$600,000 worth of assets (your home and an investment property), both growing at an average of 7% per year, for 20 years.

Investment Growth

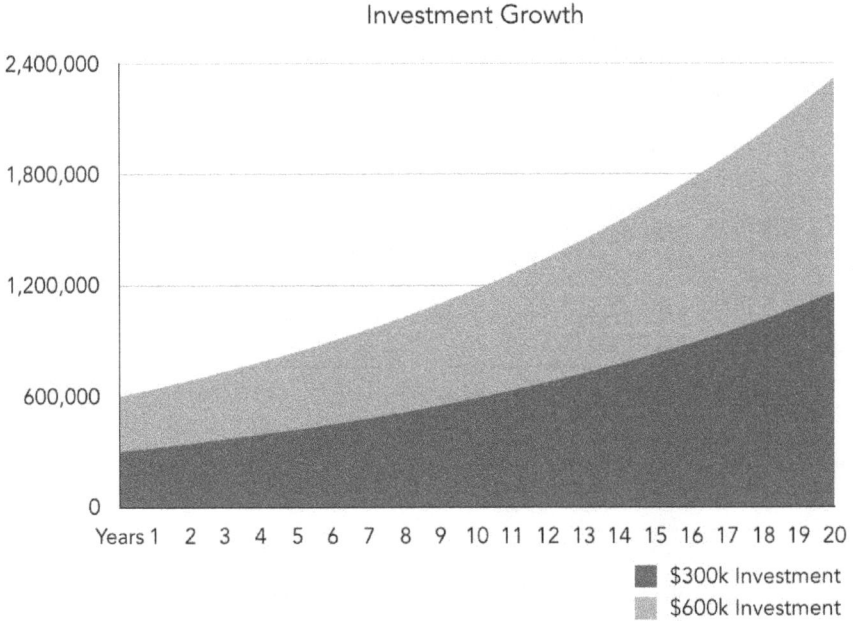

The key aspect of all of this is *effort*. You can focus your effort on paying off a mortgage of $300,000 over 10 or 20 years and end up with a property worth around $1.2 million. Or you can focus on building up more investments and end up with $2.3 million in assets with a debt of $600,000 making your solvency worth $1.8 million.

Here's an example using property.

Debt Reduction Vs Investment Accumulation Over 30 years

Focus	Debt Reduction	Increasing Solvency (Accumulating Assets)			
Asset	Home	Home	Investment Property #1	Investment Property #2	Total
Loan Type	Principal & Interest†	Interest Only	Interest Only	Interest Only	
Value (Today)	$ 300,000	$ 300,000			$ 300,000
Debt	$ (300,000)	$ (300,000)			$ (300,000)
Equity	$ 0	$ 0			$ 0
Value (in 10 years)	$ 590,145	$ 590,145	$ 500,000		$ 1,090,145
Debt	$ (237,111)	$ (300,000)	$ (500,000)		$ (800,000)
Equity	$ 353,034	$ 290,145	$ 0		$ 290,145
Value (in 20 years)	$ 1,160,905	$ 1,160,905	$ 983,576	$ 900,000	$ 3,044,481
Debt	$ (134,670)	$ (300,000)	$ (500,000)	$ (900,000)	$ (1,700,000)
Equity	$ 1,026,235	$ 860,905	$ 483,576	$ 0	$ 1,344,481
Value (in 30 years)	$ 2,283,677	$ 2,283,677	$ 1,934,842	$ 1,770,436	$ 5,988,955
Debt	$ 0	$ (300,000)	$ (500,000)	$ (900,000)	$ (1,700,000)
Equity	$ 2,283,677	$ 1,983,677	$ 1,434,842	$ 870,436	$ 4,288,955

Assumptions:
5% Interest Rate on all loans.
†$20,000 paid per annum towards Principal & Interest Loan over 30 years.
Property Growth 7% per annum.

The above table compares the difference between paying off your home and accumulating two additional investment properties. By paying interest only, the investor is able to afford another investment property. In this example the investor accumulates one extra property every

— 71 —

10 years (this is extremely conservative, two extra properties could be acquired much quicker than that). The numbers show that a substantial difference in solvency has been created with the addition of more investments. The home owner who focused on debt reduction has a solvency of $2.28 million whereas the investor who focused on *increasing* has a solvency of $4.28 million—a difference of $2 million over 30 years.

Acquiring the additional two properties requires a little more effort than just paying more off the mortgage. Once this is done, however, the solvency grows faster with minimal effort.

Focusing on increasing your solvency provides you with the choice, in the future, of selling some of your investments and paying off all your debt. Such an action would not change your solvency, but would markedly improve your viability. The effort in paying off the debt in this fashion, years from now, is very little because time has increased the asset values for you.

If you happen to be a home owner, working hard to pay off your debt, please don't feel like you've made a mistake. Any achievement you have made, whether it's a small dent in your mortgage or it's totally paid off, is truly an amazing result and I commend you for your efforts. To pursue the goal of reducing your mortgage and taking the action necessary shows that when you put your mind to it, you can achieve your goals.

My intention here is to not to discredit anyone's efforts in reducing their debt. My intention is to show you a faster way to prosperity. In the end, the choice is yours. If you sleep better at night with less investments and less debt, that's okay with me. On the other hand, if you want to build a large portfolio as soon as you can, you now have a better understanding of what to focus on. Either way, make sure you use debt for the purpose of investing and enjoy the journey!

7

YOUR SOLVENCY AND VIABILITY

The purpose of this chapter is to show you how to calculate your solvency and viability. Before you quickly work out these numbers, let's define these terms so you calculate correctly!

Calculating your solvency requires you to know the total value of your assets and debt.

Assets Defined

The dictionary defines "assets" as *a useful or valuable thing*. This is not the right definition for our use. It also defines it as *something valuable belonging to a person or organization that can be used for the payment of debts*. This is a little bit better but not exactly what we want. The word "asset" actually comes from a Latin word which means *enough* and originally meant *any property that can be converted to money*. With this understanding, we can more clearly define the word "asset."

Assets are anything that has the potential to increase in value or provide an income and can be easily sold and converted to cash.

Type of Assets

To get an accurate value of your assets, it's important that you do **not** include items that are not easily converted to money. TVs, desktop computers and clothes, while valuable to you, usually get very little in a fire sale.

Therefore, true assets are those things that increase in value and/or provide and an income *others* consider valuable.

Here's a simple list:

1. Cash

2. Property

3. Shares

4. Jewelry

5. Artwork (Collectables)

6. Antiques

7. Cars (that are roadworthy and licensed)

This list could be extended, as long as it is a genuine asset per the Rich Habits' definition. Anything else should be excluded when calculating your solvency.

When listing your assets, it's important that you put down the current market value. This might be more or less than what you paid for it. Don't put down what you think it is worth; if you are uncertain, get a professional opinion from someone in the industry or check online for similar items and what they are selling for. Always err on the side of caution when adding up your assets; you want a realistic figure not an inflated one.

Debt Defined

We know there are two types of debt but when we mention "total debt," we are referring to all your debt: both investment debt and killer debt.

"Debt" is *money you owe to others.* The original Latin word *debere* meant simply *to owe.* This includes every outstanding bill, credit card, personal loan, car loan—everything you owe! You must include all debt, even money you owe friends or family, which sometimes gets left out because it's "not a real debt." You need to include those too and add it all up.

— RICH HABITS DEFINITION —

Debt is what you owe.

Solvency

Once you know the value of your assets and your total debt, simply apply the formula for calculating your solvency.

— RICH HABITS FORMULA —

Solvency = value of assets less total debt

Now you need to put it on a graph, like the sample provided on the following page, which is included in the *Rich Habits Toolkit,* available from the website.

Solvency

Solvency

Date

Available in the *Rich Habits Toolkit*

If you are insolvent, be sure to highlight zero on the graph with a thick horizontal line so you know what you are aiming for as your primary target. If you are solvent, then set yourself a goal of increasing it to a certain level by a particular date.

Along the bottom of the graph is the date, and each square could represent a month. There are 24 squares, so that means this graph could represent 2 years.

I recommend you put the graph in a place where you will see it daily. Put it on your fridge, desk or somewhere more private, like your bathroom mirror. By putting it there, you can see your actual situation and your progress. As you see it rising, you'll also feel good about it.

Viability

Alongside your solvency graph is your viability graph. This should be graphed at the same interval as when you are paid. If you are paid weekly, then graph it weekly; if you are paid fortnightly, then do it fortnightly and so on.

— RICH HABITS FORMULA —

Viability = income is greater than or equal to your expenses

To accurately calculate your viability, we need to ensure you have the right definition for "income" and "expenses."

Income

"Income" is *all the money you received in a given time period*, whether weekly, fortnightly or monthly. You cannot count money that someone has promised you; only count the money you actually have in your hand and in your bank account. This is your total income for that time period.

Expenses

The word "expense" is defined as *money spent no something*. It originates from Latin and means literally *spent or payout.*

To calculate your expenses, take an average of everything you have spent money on over the last 3 months. Use your bank statement to get an accurate figure.

Don't include killer debt (credit card payments or overdue bills), as these are handled differently (I'll explain how later).

Here's an example of typical household expenses.

Living Expenses

Living Expenses	Amount Spent (Every week, bi-weekly or monthly)
Food & Groceries	
Rent/Mortgage Payments	
Travel (fuel, train ticket, etc)	
Utilities (Electricity, Gas, Water)	
Telephone	
Clothing	
Car Expense (Maintenance, etc)	
Insurances	
Internet Services	
Children's Education Fees	
Car Payments	
Investment Loan Payments	
Total	$

Available in the *Rich Habits Toolkit*

Viability Graph

Plot both your income and expenses on the same graph.

Viability

Amount
$

| Income |
| --- Expenses |

Date

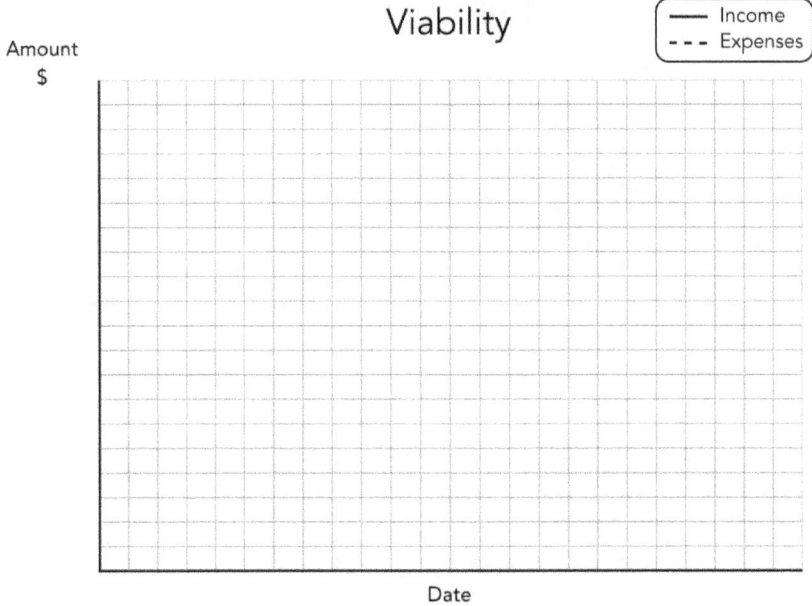

Available in the *Rich Habits Toolkit*

It's important to graph this regularly so you keep track of your viability and don't spend more than you make. You can grab your copy of the graph above from the *Rich Habits Toolkit*.

8
HOW TO CONTROL MONEY

△

This is, perhaps, the most important chapter in the book. This is where you learn the art of money control.

No matter how much money you make, or how insolvent you are, the skill of controlling money is vital to your survival and long-term prosperity.

In this chapter, you will learn how to fly; you will earn your financial wings.

Time and Money

When you think about it, money problems are really a problem of "too little money and too little time." An overdue bill is one that has run out of time. If there was more time to pay the bill, then only the lack of money is the problem. So time and money go together; they seem to affect each other.

You can split "time" up into 3 basic categories: past, present and future. We all have a past, present and future. Each of these "time" categories must be provided for financially. Failure to provide for the past, present and future is the main cause of financial difficulty.

Let me explain.

Assume you have $500 cash. That's all the money you have right now, and you won't be paid any more money for another week. Let's say you spent all that money on a fun night out with friends! You didn't buy any groceries for the following week, and you spent your rent money and fuel money too. Now you have no money left for the future.

Spending Future Money

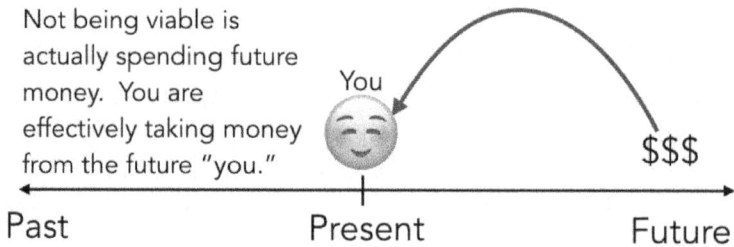

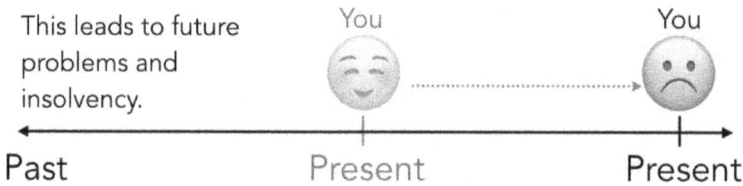

Not being viable is actually spending future money. You are effectively taking money from the future "you."

You

$$$

Past Present Future

This leads to future problems and insolvency.

You You

Past Present Present

The result of spending future money means the future becomes harder to live. You will have to borrow money to survive until the next paycheck arrives. This, in turn, takes more from your future money—and so the spiral begins. The more you use your future money to live today, the harder the future becomes to live.

When you overspend today, no matter who you borrow

it from, you are taking from your future self. And you do so without permission or the good manners to even ask— you just take it. When you take something without asking for it, it's called *stealing*. So, being unviable is the same as *stealing from your future self.*

Using future money makes you insolvent and makes you a slave. The "older you" in the future is paying for the "younger you." It makes the future harder. If time travel were possible, I'm sure one of its uses would be to go back in time and warn ourselves to avoid certain situations. On the top of the list would be a visit to the "younger you" with a stern request to tighten spending habits (and maybe a copy of this book)!

Let's take a look at a better approach. Instead of spending all of your $500 paycheck, organize your finances to provide money for today and for the future. As an example, the $500 could be allocated as follows:

Example Allocation Table

Item	Amount
Rent	$190
Food	$90
Fuel	$45
Fun	$50
Investing	$100
Emergencies	$25
Total	**$500**

Available in the *Rich Habits Toolkit*

You can still enjoy a fun night with your friends, but spending is limited to $50. The rest is allocated for a specific purpose, as above.

Now you have a future and it's worth living. The more you do this, the brighter the future looks and is. Your solvency will increase.

But what if you're already insolvent? How do you pay off the old debt? This is where the past comes in.

Any debt or unpaid bill you have is in the past—it's old. The older it is, the more trouble it gives you. Therefore, you want to get rid of old, unpaid debt. It's killer debt because it is old and unpaid.

Your financial control system needs to take into account old debt so it gets paid off.

The following Rich Habits Allocation method is one that works because it caters to the past, present and future.

Firstly, which do you think is the most important: the past, present or future? The correct answer is the future. Those who have no future are miserable. The stress suffered by students at the end of school exams is nothing more than the fear of not having a future. If they only realized that such exams are not the be-all and end-all, I think students would feel less stressed and possibly get better grades.

The future is more important and the first thing that must be catered for. Always allocate a percentage of your income for the future. Then you take a portion for the past: the killer debt. Next, allocate money for emergencies —this is "just in case" something unexpected happens. The rest is what you use to live.

You might think this is simply saving money, but it is not. This is very different to saving money because for most people, saving doesn't work.

Why Saving Doesn't Work

We've all tried to save money at some point. I find that the only ones who succeed at it hide the money. The majority of us can't seem to save.

Have you ever found $10 or $20 in a pocket of some clothes you haven't worn for a while? It's a great surprise when you do, but no sooner found, it is spent. Why is that?

It seems that money was meant to flow freely through society from one person to the next. We all know that if we left $50 on the street, it would not be there for long: it would travel from one hand to the next rather quickly!

The reason saving doesn't work is because money is meant to be spent. The dictionary defines money as a *medium of exchange*. It is *supposed to* change hands, from one person to the next. Trying to hold on to it is like trying to hold back the tide: it was never designed to stay in one place.

Then how do you go about keeping money so you can provide for the future? The answer is quite simple.

Money needs a *purpose*. Money without a purpose disappears. The one who gives money a purpose becomes its master. Money without a purpose is like an orphan child with no master.

A Master of Money builds up tremendous wealth when money is given a specific purpose that is *never* violated.

The "secret" to controlling money is this: *Money must have a purpose*. When money is received, the Money Master must separate it into its assigned purposes. This creates a future and abundance.

This is not saving. Most saving is simply money put aside for the future but with no real purpose in mind. A true Money Master not only sets aside money but *clearly defines* the purpose for that money. And once the purpose is clearly defined, the money is used for nothing else other than that purpose. We call this "allocating" and it's another fundamental Rich Habit and it has a specific definition.

— Rich Habits Definition —

Allocate means separating money for a specific purpose and using it only for that purpose.

When money is not assigned a purpose, it's gets spent. Spending without a plan is a Poor Habit.

— Rich Habit —

The Rich always allocate.

— Poor Habit —

The Poor spend without plan.

There is no limit to the number of purposes you can assign money, whether it's for the past, present or future. The important thing to remember is *always* allocate each purpose to it's own bank account; keep them separate. The absolute minimum allocations you should be aiming for, are described below in order of importance.

Investment Allocation

This money is to be used only to buy appreciating assets which include property, shares and businesses, to name a few. It cannot be used for any other purpose. Once the investments are purchased, any loan repayments (such as a mortgage) must come from the Living Allocation.

Killer Debt Allocation

Investments are an allocation for the *future*, whereas killer debt is an expense from the *past*. If you have any type of killer debt (such as credit cards or overdue bills), you must allocate money for this purpose and use that money to eliminate your killer debt. Follow the principles outlined in this book and swim to the surface like mad until you are solvent. Once solvent, and free of killer debt, you no longer need a Killer Debt Allocation!

Living Allocation

This is your money for the present, the "now." Use it to pay for your general expenses, the vital ones we covered earlier including mortgage payments, rent, food, clothes, etc. For a business, it could be called "fixed costs."

Education Allocation

The day you stop learning is the day you die! Your Education Allocation is used to pay for your continued education. This can be any type of education as long as it improves you as a person. Anything from a university degree to an investment seminar or book can be purchased with this money. Don't let the balance become too big; spend it on education and never stop learning!

Emergency Allocation

Consider this your own personal insurance fund. It is an allocation for the *future*. The money can be used to pay for any medical expenses resulting from illnesses or accidents. If such an illness or accident affects your income, this money can be used to help pay for living expenses until insurance payments are received or you are back on your feet again. Family emergencies are also included in this. Damage to property can be paid for using these funds. It cannot be used to pay out a debt—that is not an emergency.

Fun Allocation

If you neglect to spend time with your spouse or children, they'll eventually begin to resent you working hard. If you have ever managed staff, you'll know that acknowledgement of a job well done goes a long way, often more than a bonus check.

The same applies to you: don't neglect yourself. You too deserve a reward for your efforts. No matter how hard you work or how deep you are swimming, allocate some funds to a Fun Allocation and remember to take some time to have a little fun.

It makes the rest of the week worthwhile and provides a sense of accomplishment.

Everyone deserves a little fun. Even you.

Allocate

Allocate: to separate money for a specific purpose
and use it only for that purpose.

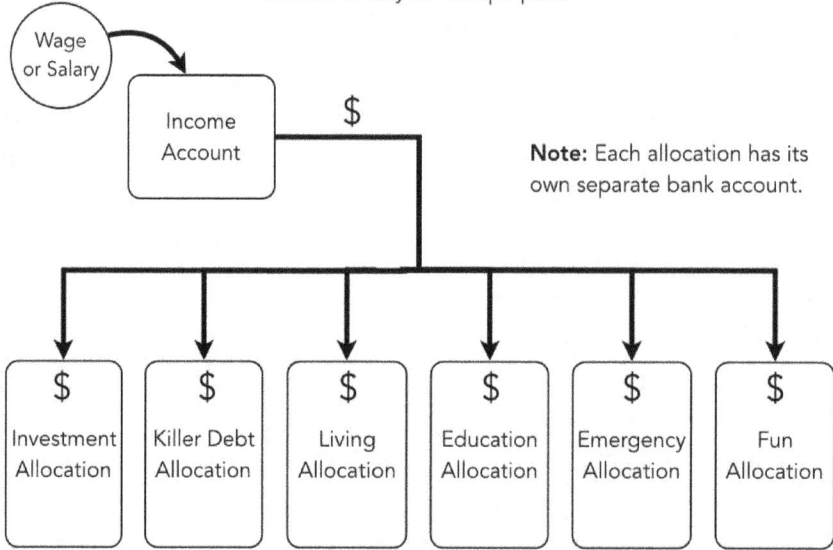

```
  Wage
or Salary
      ↓
   Income          $
   Account
                        Note: Each allocation has its
                        own separate bank account.

   $        $        $        $        $        $
Investment KillerDebt Living  Education Emergency  Fun
Allocation Allocation Allocation Allocation Allocation Allocation
```

It may seem impossible to put money aside for all of these different purposes and still have enough to live. But spending everything you make without providing for the future is simply a Poor Habit. Remember, the rich *always* allocate.

Bank Accounts

You will need separate bank accounts for each of the allocations mentioned above. Do <u>not</u> keep the money in a single account because it is too easy to accidentally use money for the wrong purpose.

You'll find that banks, strangely enough, might

discourage the idea of opening so many bank accounts. Often, you'll run into opposition from accountants too. In this case, ignore both; go ahead and establish a separate account for each fund. It makes it easier for you to control your money.

I personally have a separate account for income, making a total of seven accounts. Having an Income Account makes it very easy to see how much money was made in a given week or month. When it comes time to allocate any money received for the week, it's a matter of transferring all the money from the Income Account into the respective accounts, as illustrated above.

One of the reasons people avoid separate bank accounts is because of the extra cost of bank fees. Even some banks will warn you about this! My advice is don't worry about the bank fees; simply ask your bank for low-fee or no-fee accounts. Every account except the Living Allocation fund has very little transactions and therefore minimal fees. As the balance builds up in your Investment and Emergency accounts, the interest you receive is more than all the bank fees you pay, especially if you use high interest accounts for those allocations.

These are the different bank accounts you need.

Bank Accounts

	Account Name	Type	Number of Transactions	Balance
1	Income	Savings	Moderate 6 - 25 per month	Funds used regularly
2	Investment	Savings	Minimal 1 - 4 per month	Growing balance, high interest
3	Killer Debt	Checking	Minimal 1 - 4 per month	Steady balance, moderate use
4	Living	Checking	Many 30+ per month	Funds used regularly
5	Emergency	Savings	Minimal 1 - 4 per month	Growing balance, high interest
6	Education	Savings	Minimal 1 - 4 per month	Steady balance, moderate use
7	Fun	Savings	Moderate 6 - 25 per month	Funds used regularly

Just how much of your income do you allocate for each purpose? It depends where you lie on the Rich Continuum, which we'll cover in the next chapter.

9

THE RICH CONTINUUM

In the last few chapters, we covered the three most fundamental Rich Habits you need to follow to be Rich, these are:

1. The Rich are **solvent** and constantly improve it.

2. The Rich are *always* **viable**.

3. The Rich *always* **allocate**.

These Rich Habits form the foundation of wealth. They are inseparable. They work together. If you fail on any of these, it adversely affects the other two. If you apply all three, you will be Rich.

Rich Triangle

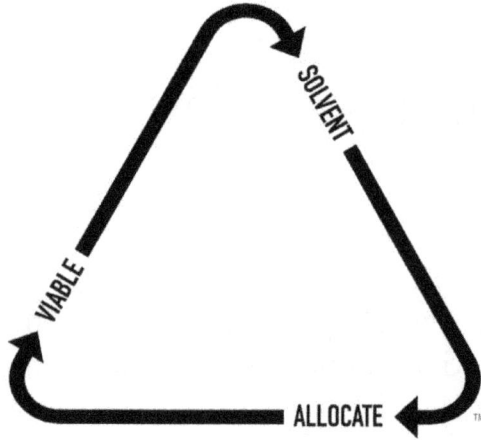

As you can see by the illustration above, each Rich Habit flows to the next. The first step is to *allocate*, which leads to being *viable* which in turn leads to being more *solvent*. Fail on any one and it will affect the flow. While the ultimate goals are to be both solvent and viable, the first *action* taken is always to *allocate*. The Rich Triangle is a tool to use to remind yourself of the simple steps you need to be Rich.

Every positive has a negative, there is good and evil, and there is, unfortunately an opposite to the Rich Triangle—it's the Poor Triangle. It is, however, worthwhile to understand the Poor Triangle, for it provides an awareness of what must be avoided, so that one never falls into financial difficulty again.

The Poor Triangle comprises the 3 most fundamental Poor Habits:

1. The Poor don't allocate; they **spend**.

2. The Poor tolerate being **unviable**.

3. The Poor tolerate being **insolvent**.

Thus, we have the elements of the Poor Triangle.

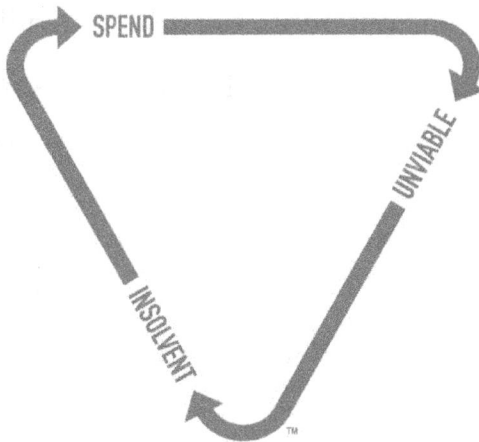

Poor Triangle

SPEND

UNVIABLE

INSOLVENT

To be Rich requires that you cease practicing Poor Habits and replace them with Rich Habits.

The Rich Continuum

A *continuum* is a continuous sequence in which adjacent elements are not perceptibly different from each other, although the extremes are quite distinct. Life is a continuum, with each passing day we all get a little older. We hardly notice it, but when you see a photo of yourself taken a decade ago, you appear noticeably younger. This is very easily seen in children. Close family and friends who see the child regularly hardly notice the changes as the child grows. But relatives and friends who see the child once a year notice, the change is dramatic and obvious. In the continuum of life, the small daily changes are barely noticeable, but the difference overtime is significant.

When we place the Rich Triangle on top of the Poor Triangle we have the Rich Continuum.

The Rich Continuum™

The difference between Rich and Poor is dramatic and obvious, but the subtle shifts from the top to the bottom are barely noticeable unless you practice the Rich Habits.

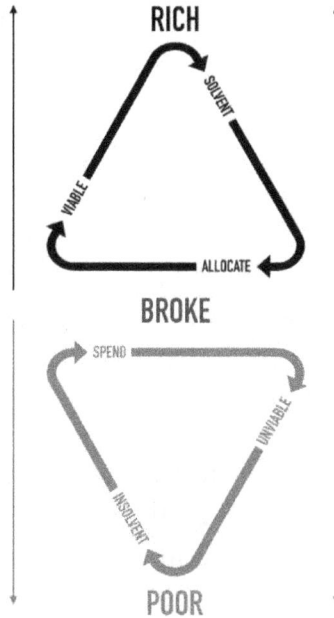

The Rich Continuum is a continuous sequence or journey from Poor to Rich in which adjacent levels are not perceptibly different from each other, although the extremes are quite distinct and obvious. Understanding the Rich Continuum explains many things, for example: Countries, companies and individuals don't suddenly go broke, nor do they suddenly become rich. They move on the Rich Continuum everyday, up or down. Most do so unknowingly, yet everyone is somewhere on the Rich Continuum. You are sitting somewhere between Rich and Poor, and every day you move either slightly higher or slightly lower.

Right in the middle of the Rich Continuum is the status of *Broke*, where a person has zero solvency; they are neither insolvent, nor solvent. They have no assets and no debt.

Or perhaps, they have lots of assets, but they also have lots of debt, so the end result is zero. The dictionary defines "broke" as *having completely run out of money*. And this is how they live, week to week, month to month. They continually "run out of money" by spending all their income. They might even spend a bit more than they earn. The end result is zero. There are a lot of people living in a fancy house, with fancy cars who are in fact Broke, and they sit unknowingly right in the middle of the Rich Continuum, which is a very dangerous place to be.

The start of any journey requires two things; first, a destination (a goal); second, a journey requires you know exactly where you are, so you know which direction to go. Our financial goal is to head toward Rich—to be viable and solvent. Finding out exactly where you are on the Rich Continuum is the next step. By knowing exactly where you are, you also know exactly what you need to do. If you are insolvent, you are in the Poor Triangle and you need to get solvent. If you are close to Broke, neither solvent or insolvent, then you sit right in the middle, and there are certain steps you need to take to move up into the Rich Triangle. If you are solvent, you are in the Rich Triangle and by applying the Rich Habits, you'll never fall back down again—you'll simply get richer and richer.

Our ocean and sky analogy still applies. The Poor Triangle is completely underwater where desperate beings battle with debt collectors while holding their breath until the next paycheck. Broke is at the water level, where people will tread endlessly in a state of financial anxiety, worried that they might suddenly slip under the surface. The Rich Triangle sits in the sky where people are free to roam and go where they please. The Rich Continuum maps the journey and shows you the way to a life free of financial stress and worry, a life of financial abundance.

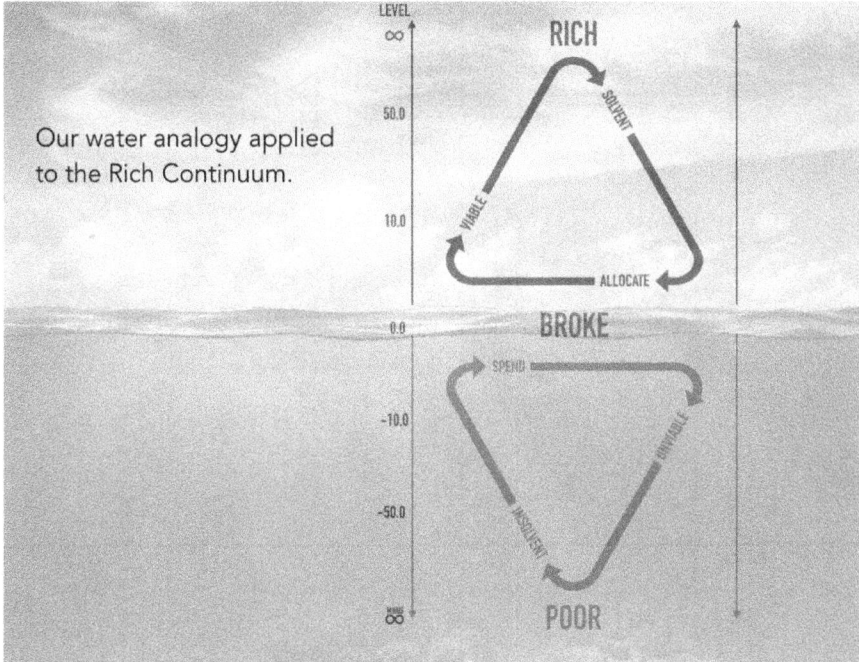

Our water analogy applied to the Rich Continuum.

Rich Continuum Chart

I have created the following chart that identifies the key characteristics at each level of the Rich Continuum. It will help you easily identify where you are on the Rich Continuum, so you can proactively improve your situation immediately by raising your position in each column. It is a tool that you use to move away from Poor and closer to Rich. You can apply this chart to yourself and your business. It's is included in the *Rich Habits Toolkit* and is available for free from myrichhabits.com.

THE RICH CONTINUUM*

Rich Level		A — Awareness of Rich Habits	B — Allocation	C — Viability	D — Solvency	E — Financial Attention (Time)	F — Goals & Problems	G — Opportunity	H — Identification of Friends & Foes	I — Proactiveness & Blame	J — Negotiation
		Rich Habits				**Focus**			**Skills & Abilities**		
RICH	∞	Practices Rich Habits naturally.	Allocates more than True Allocation, always.	Abundantly Viable. Has surplus.	Abundantly Solvent.	Long-term future.	Long-term goals.	Sees and takes advantage of unlimited opportunities.	Lots of supportive solvent friends. No foes.	Responds quickly and effectively to situations. Rarely engages in blame.	Knows that everything and anything is negotiable and does so with creativity and certainty so that everyone wins.
	50.0	Knows and practices Rich Habits.	True Allocation.	Constantly improving viability.	Increasing Solvency; zero Killer Debt.	Short-term future.	Short-terms goals.	Starts to see and explore more opportunities.	Few supportive friends. Foes, if any, have little effective.	Looks for ways to be proactive.	Willing and able to negotiate successfully.
	10.0	Learning and beginning to follow Rich Habits.	Basic Allocation.	Viable, but not yet with True Allocation.	Becoming more solvent.	Immediate future.	Striving for True Allocation and Solvency.	Tentatively looks and explores new opportunities.	Identified friends, eliminating foes.	Aware of the difference between blaming and responding. Starting to be proactive.	Attempts to negotiate and starts to succeed.
BROKE	0.0	Unaware of Rich Habits.	Very basic allocation, if any.	Spends all income when received.	The value of any assets, if owned, are nullified by debt.	Now.	Little focus, stuck in a never-ending financial uncertainty.	Seldom sees opportunities.	Unknown association with Foes.	Decisive responsive actions are seldom. Operates on whim or demands of others.	Seldom negotiates.
	-10.0	Practices Poor Habits.	Allocates haphazardly, usually to the most urgent or demanding bill.	Living expenses equal to or more than income.	Some Killer Debt.	Recent Past.	Worried about income and bills.	Too worried to see opportunities.	Has "friends" that are really foes.	Takes little proactive action. Likely to blame others.	Doesn't negotiate.
	-50.0	Thinks you have to be lucky to be rich.	Cannot allocate. Uses debt to pay bills.	Spends more than income. Wasteful.	Insolvent. May try to appear "Rich" through the use of Killer Debt.	Past (months to years).	Lots of money problems.	Only sees "Get Rich Quick" opportunities. Misses genuine opportunities.	Foes actively and unknowingly working against the individual.	Blames other people, organizations and government for all difficulties. Feels overwhelmed by those blamed. Not proactive.	Does not believe negotiation is possible. Waits for something to be less expensive. Compromises.
POOR	-∞	Helplessly and hopelessly practices Poor Habits.	Income seized by debt collectors (forced allocation).	Unviable. Income cannot cover living expenses and debt repayments.	Bankrupt or on the verge of being so.	Past (many years).	Overwhelming money problems. Believes there is no way out.	Likely to be skeptical of any opportunity.	Foes have succeeded in the destruction of the individual and their dreams. Foes abandon the individual, only friends remain.	Everything that happens is somebody else's fault. Tries unsuccessfully to fight those blamed (lawsuits).	Might try to negotiate by being dishonest in a desperate attempt to win.

*Definition: **Continuum** — a continuous sequence in which adjacent elements are not perceptibly different from each other, although the extremes are quite distinct.

Available in the *Rich Habits Toolkit*

The Rich Levels

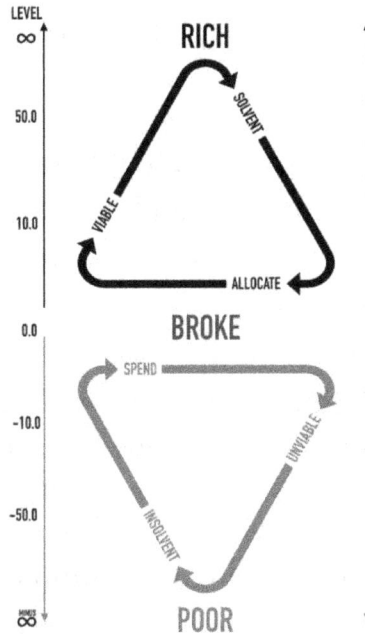

Numbers assigned to different stages of the Rich Continuum are used to easily identify the major "Rich Levels."

Each Rich Level has exact steps to move the individual or business upwards.

The numbers on the Rich Continuum are arbitrary numbers assigned to identify the different levels. Broke is at 0.0, right in the middle. As we move up, 10.0 represents someone starting to practice Rich Habits, getting more solvent and viable. At 50.0, they are well on their way and have eliminated all killer debt. The last level is represented by the infinity symbol "∞" because there is truly no limit to how Rich you can be.

Below broke we have the Rich level of -10.0 where a person is practicing Poor Habits, has killer debts, is not viable and is worried about money. At -50.0, they are really sinking deeper and have lots of money problems.

This scale provides a method of identifying where a

person, business or country lies on the Rich Continuum, and we designate it simply by "Rich 10.0" or "Rich -50.0," as the case may be. Even though a person or business may sit in the Poor Triangle at -50.0, I refer to their level as "Rich -50.0" and not "Poor -50.0" because the designation "Rich -50.0" reminds a person they are on the Rich Continuum, and no matter how low they have fallen, they can still climb back up. It keeps everyone's focus on the positive goal.

At the bottom of the Rich Continuum is the level of *minus* infinity "-∞." Surprisingly, there is no limit to how Poor (insolvent and unviable) a person, business or country can become. You have heard stories of people stealing or losing millions, even billions, of investors' money from a company, sending that company into complete insolvency. And what about Greece in 2016? As a result of Poor Habits at the government level, it was so overburdened with debt, it could not afford to make any repayments. Yet what did Greece do to get out of the killer debt she had accumulated? How did Greece move up the Rich Continuum and resolve the financial problems of her country? She didn't. The "solution" to overwhelming killer debt as a nation was simple. After many meetings with politicians and international banks, these incredibly bright individuals managed to "solve" the "debt" problem with more debt! How's that for Poor Habits? Thus, the Rich Continuum is limitless in both directions.

Needless to say, misery sits in the lower part and the the deeper one travels, the more miserable, difficult and cutthroat life becomes. Thankfully, true happiness, joy and fun do exist, but these are reserved for those *above* the level of Broke, who have no money problems and are rich enough to help their fellow man.

The Poor Plague

The money system and society at large are designed to keep the majority of people at the level of Broke or below.

This is not a conspiracy theory—just take a look around. Try to find a solvent country. Look at the rising national debt. Listen to a conversation of another in a cafe and you will notice a comment or two about money problems. Visit ten local businesses in your area, and the majority will be found to have cash-flow problems, tax debts and unpaid bills.

Poor Habits are a plague, so it's no surprise that many suffer, but if the Rich Habits are well known and taught, we can change the tide, and move more and more people up the Rich Continuum, if you help me spread the word. After all, today's children will be tomorrow's leaders. How can they practice Rich Habits if all they know are Poor Habits?

The key to moving up the Rich Continuum is to know the *Laws of Allocation,* the topic of the next chapter.

10

THE LAWS OF ALLOCATION

I have helped many individuals and business owners implement the Rich Habits. The biggest hurdle to overcome is not killer debt or dealing with disgruntled creditors, as one might suspect. The biggest hurdle is allocating correctly.

The reason this step is so difficult has nothing to do with intelligence. Everyone from doctors to accountants have difficulty with this step. The reason it is so difficult is due to the confusion of the term "income."

During my business career, I have been a part owner in three different accounting firms (despite not been an accountant!). As such, I've heard plenty of accountant jokes in my time. I'm reminded of one particular joke that is quite fitting.

Joe is an astute businessman and decides he needs to find a proactive accountant. He has three recommended accountants on his list and meets each accountant separately. Joe explains to each accountant the following: "I need to hire a proactive accountant. I'm going to ask you one simple question, and your answer to this question will determine whether or not I hire you."

He asks the first accountant, "What is two plus two?" The accountant replies without any delay, "Ha, that's easy; it's four!"

Joe thanks him and goes to his next meeting.

Accountant number 2 is asked, "What is two plus two?" To Joe's surprise, the accountant pulls out a calculator and starts rapidly hitting the keys. After several minutes, he looks up with a triumphant grin and replies, "It's 3.9999 recurring."

Joe thanks him and goes to his next meeting.

At the final meeting with accountant number 3, Joe asks, "What is two plus two?" The accountant smiles, crosses his hand as he leans on the desk and whispers to Joe, "What would *you* like it to be?"

And that is why finance is so confusing. It's a great gag, but it is also very factual. The definition of income and the treatment of debts and expenses have all been twisted and made unnecessarily complex and very confusing.

As a very simple example, ask anyone what they get paid, and most will tell you their *gross salary*. Rarely do people quote their pay *after* tax—what they actually receive.

Two Types of Income

A trick of sorts has been played on those who earn money—both individuals and corporations, big and small. The trick and the basic confusion of money troubles is this: *not all the money you receive belongs to you.*

There are two types of income. The money you receive falls into two categories: the money you can *use* and the money you *can't use*. The money you can't use is income that does <u>not</u> belong to you.

If you take a look at any payslip you will see something like this: Weekly income $1,000, Tax withheld $200, Net income $800 (this is what the person actually receives).

The tax portion is *unusable income.* You don't receive it, but you did earn it. Many assume that *all* the amount received, the $800, is usable income, but this is not always the case. For example, if you have to pay child support, education debts or past taxes, these obligations are often enforced by strict laws—they must be removed before any other allocations occur.

The two types of income are most prevalent in business, where money received includes sales tax, profit tax, cost of goods, staff wages, sales commissions—the income to cover these obligations is unusable income. If spent it leads the business into trouble because that income does not belong to the business.

Types of Income
Each circle represents total money received

Personal   Business

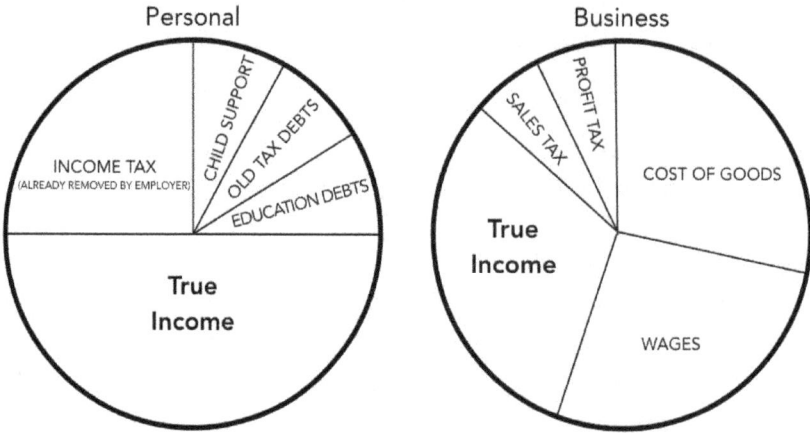

INCOME TAX
(ALREADY REMOVED BY EMPLOYER)

CHILD SUPPORT

OLD TAX DEBTS

EDUCATION DEBTS

True
Income

PROFIT TAX

SALES TAX

COST OF GOODS

True
Income

WAGES

Only True Income can be used.
Unusable Income must be removed before Allocation occurs.

Just like the English language fails to define the two different types of debt (investment debt and killer debt), so too are we left with only *one word*—"income," to describe the types of money received, when in fact there are two types of income.

There are plenty of words used by accountants and governments to describe income, but we certainly don't want to use any of those terms because they are apt to change, to make profits more, or less, depending on who is receiving the report.

We need new and simple terms that will help you allocate correctly and apply the Rich Habits.

The types of "income" are:

1. **Money Received** - the total amount of money received for a given period, such as a week or month.

2. **Unusable Income** - Money Received that does not belong to you and must be set aside *before* any other allocations occur.

3. **True Income** - the remainder leftover from Money Received, after Unusable Income has been removed.

With the above definitions the formula for True Income is easy to follow:

— RICH HABITS FORMULA —

True Income = Money Received less Unusable Income

Allocation Process

Therefore, Allocation is a three-step process:

1. Work out total Money Received.

2. Remove the Unusable Income (each to its own bank account).

3. The remainder, the True Income, is then allocated into its specific accounts.

The following table shows examples of calculating True Income for an individual and a business.

True Income Calculation Examples

Personal Allocation	
Money Received	**$2,000**
Less Child Support	-$500
Less Education Debt	-$100
Less Old Tax Debt	-$100
True Income	**$1,300**

Business Allocation	
Money Received	**$10,000**
Less Sales Tax	-$1,000
Less Cost of Goods	-$3,000
Less Wages	-$3,000
Less Profit Tax	-$1,000
True Income	**$2,000**

The following illustration demonstrates the entire Allocation Process.

The Entire Allocation Process

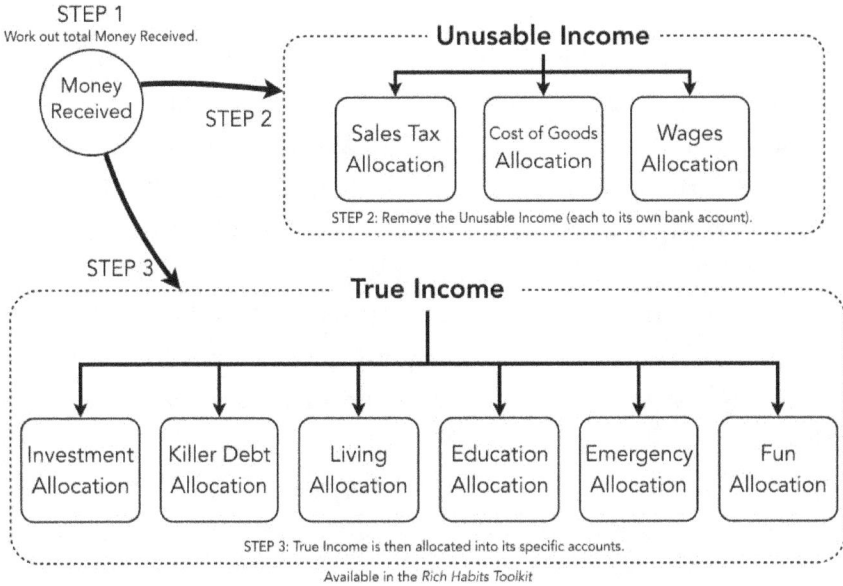

STEP 1
Work out total Money Received.

Unusable Income

Money Received

STEP 2

| Sales Tax Allocation | Cost of Goods Allocation | Wages Allocation |

STEP 2: Remove the Unusable Income (each to its own bank account).

STEP 3

True Income

| Investment Allocation | Killer Debt Allocation | Living Allocation | Education Allocation | Emergency Allocation | Fun Allocation |

STEP 3: True Income is then allocated into its specific accounts.

Available in the *Rich Habits Toolkit*

Allocation Table

Every elite athlete first started as a novice, incrementally improving until at last they break through, into the realm of a professional, where they achieve outstanding feats that us mere mortals consider impossible. The same applies to a business executive who can build and command an entire company all in the same 8 or 9 hours a day that some of us struggle to get even the most basic tasks done. The singer and songwriter can belt out a tune that makes us dance or weep, and often they do it with their eyes closed, hardly even looking at their instruments or referring to a score.

Were they born that way? Rarely. We often only see such individuals at the peak of their accomplishments;

unseen is the climb to the top, which is done one step at a time.

Moving up the Rich Continuum is no different. The journey from the bottom to the top should not be measured in time. Measure it instead by your steady progress towards solvency. Needless to say, the journey from *Broke* to *Rich* is much shorter than it is from *Poor* to *Rich*, and therefore the approach is slightly different. And although it may sound a little funny, being Broke is a lot better than being Poor. I recall reaching the status of Broke (Rich 0.0) where my solvency was zero. It was exhilarating, but it's not something you can really brag about ("Yippee I'm Broke!") Perhaps one day, when more people learn about the Rich Continuum, it won't sound like such a silly statement.

If you happen to find yourself in the Poor Triangle, towards the bottom of the Rich Continuum, just like I was, you need to allocate differently than when you are in the Rich Triangle. The main focus, when underwater, is to eliminate all killer debt as soon as you can and head upwards, towards solvency.

As you progress upwards and move towards the center of the Rich Continuum, you can adjust your allocations to further speed up your journey. Once free from the burden of killer debt, you'll find you can soar upwards much faster.

With that in mind, the following Allocation Table provides a guide to the percentage of True Income that should be allocated.

Rich Habits Allocation Table

Percentage of True Income allocated at different levels of the Rich Continuum

	Investment	Killer Debt	Living	Education	Emergency	Fun
Solvent without Killer Debt Rich Triangle Rich Continuum Level* 50.0 and above	20%	None	70%	5%	4%	1%
Solvent with Killer Debt Lower Rich Triangle Rich Continuum Level* 0.0 to 10.0	10%	20%	60%	5%	4%	1%
Insolvent Poor Triangle Rich Continuum Level* -10.0 and below	10%	30%	60%	None	None	Opitional

*The Rich Continuum Levels are taken from the The Rich Continuum Chart, available in the *Rich Habits Toolkit*

You can, off course, allocate more to Investments and Killer Debt if you wish, to help speed up your journey. Initially you might have to make some adjustments to your living expenses, but you'll find that if you stick to it, it becomes easier; and because you are allocating for the future, life becomes easier. With your wealth increasing, you can get addicted to seeing your solvency improve; the game becomes, "how can I allocate more?" which is a real fun game to play. And before you know it, you'll be at the top of the Rich Continuum.

Viability Formula Clarified

Answer this question honestly: Are you earning more

now than you did 5 years ago? Unless you are under 12 years old, I imagine the answer is "yes."

If you are earning more money than you were 5 years ago, then where has that extra money gone? I'll answer this for you: It has been spent. Your expenses jumped up to match your income, whether it was a new car, holiday, bigger house, a boat or simply a more extravagant lifestyle; your expenses have increased to match your income.

The Poor Habit of spending all that you make must be changed into the Rich Habit of *allocating* before spending anything. To do that requires a thorough understanding of *viability*. In the previous chapters, the formula for viability is stated as follows:

— RICH HABITS FORMULA —

Viability = income greater than or equal to your expenses

Now that understand the process of Allocation and its vital role as a component of the Rich Triangle, the actual formula for viability is changed to this:

— RICH HABITS FORMULA —

Viability = True Income is greater than or equal to your allocations

Methods of Allocation

There are two types of allocations methods. When an individual is insolvent, elimination of all killer debt is the primary focus, therefore ***Basic Allocation*** includes only:

1. Investment

2. Killer Debt

3. Living

When an individual is solvent, ***True Allocation*** includes the following; these are listed in order of priority:

1. Investment

2. Killer Debt (until eliminated)

3. Living

4. Education or Personal Development

5. Emergency

6. Fun

Always strive for True Allocation, no matter where you sit on the Rich Continuum. But at the very least you must apply the *Basic Allocation* using the *Allocation Table* above. Never settle for anything less. Covering *only* your living expenses does not mean you are viable; it's a poor habit because you are not allocating for the future or removing the burden of killer debt. To be viable, *Basic Allocation* is the bare minimum.

myrichhabits.com

— RICH HABIT —

The Rich always know the income required for True Allocation.

— POOR HABIT —

The Poor are ignorant of the income needed to allocate and be viable.

The Laws of Allocation

Allocation is an exact process. It has its own laws that are very precise. Violation of these will drive you down the Rich Continuum into the deep.

At the top of the Rich Continuum, the Rich allocate naturally; at the level of Broke, there is no allocation whatsoever, money is spent without plan and if continued, the person drops further until eventually, at the level Poor, income is seized by debt collectors, which is a method of enforced allocation by another. Therefore, it can be observed that allocation will occur and the more one violates these laws, the less control a person has over their income. Just as a person will fall if they jump from a tall building, a person who never allocates will eventually find themselves at the bottom of the Rich Continuum. On a brighter note, strict adherence to these principles will help you soar with the eagles. I can tell you, from personal experience, being at the top of the Rich Continuum is much more enjoyable, so know the laws well.

1. To **allocate** is the action of separating money for a

specific purpose and using it only for that purpose.

2. Never spend unallocated money. Always allocate before you spend.

3. Each allocation <u>must</u> have its own bank account. <u>Never</u> put money with a different purpose into the same account.

4. Allocation is a three-step process:

    -   The first step of **Allocation** is to work out how much money was received.

    -   The second step of **Allocation** is to remove **Unusable Money** (money that does not belong to you) and allocate each to its own bank account, leaving only **True Income** remaining.

    -   The third step is to allocate to all remaining **True Income.**

5. When an individual is insolvent, elimination of all killer debt is the primary focus; therefore ***Basic Personal Allocation*** includes only:

    -   Investment

    -   Killer Debt

    -   Living

6. When an individual is solvent, ***True Personal Allocation*** includes (in order of priority):

    -   Investment

- Killer Debt

- Living

- Education or Personal Development

- Emergency

- Fun

7. ***Business Allocation*** includes (in order of priority):

    - Promotion

    - Investment

    - Killer Debt

    - Business Fix Costs

    - Emergency

8. You can create an allocation for anything.

9. Choose a specific time each week to allocate.

10. If you don't have a enough income to allocate, you are not viable. Allocate to the fund that will help you increase your income or in the order of priority.

11. Borrowing money to pay bills does not make you viable; it make you less solvent and sends you tumbling down the Rich Continuum towards Poor.

12. If you are not viable, the solution is to MAKE MORE MONEY.

13. The more you allocate, the richer you become.

11

GET VIABLE

This chapter is especially for those who have discovered the sobering fact that they are unviable and are heading in the wrong direction!

You must head up the Rich Continuum, towards the sky! If you are insolvent, no matter how much debt you are in, you must swim upwards. Swimming sideways will not do and swimming deeper is deadly.

If you are not viable, then this needs to change immediately.

Get Viable Step 1 - Reduce Expenses

Reducing expenses is a necessary step towards viability, but it is limited. You cannot reduce your expenses to zero. Increasing your income on the other hand has no limits, so don't spend too much time on this. Get this step done fast and start focusing on making more money.

As mentioned earlier, first you need to know what your expenses are. Take the average of your spending over the last 3 months using your bank statements and see what you are actually spending money on. It's often a surprise to most people to discover how much things cost and how quickly "little" expenses such as eating out add up over the weeks and months.

Do not include killer debt payments in your calculation, such as monthly payments to credit card or personal loans, as these are handled separately via your Killer Debt Allocation, which we'll cover in the next chapter.

Once you have the average expenses, work out what you can reduce or eliminate, like travel costs, eating out, electricity, etc. Your goal is to reduce your living expenses below 70% of your income if you are solvent or below 60% if you are insolvent.

Get Viable Step 2 - Agreement to Be Viable

Once you have your Living Allocation at a viable level, share it with everyone involved. Make sure your spouse and children are aware of the new "family budget" and restrictions—things like making lunches, turning off the lights, catching public transport instead of driving the car. Get everyone involved and get them to agree to stick to it with the goal of improving solvency. If you are applying this to a business, do the same with key personnel in the business.

This is a vital step to ensure that overspending does not occur, and with everyone in agreement, you are now ready for the next step.

Get Viable Step 3 - Make More Money (Personal)

The next step, after reducing expenses to the viability

level, is to earn more money. There are 5 things you can do immediately:

1. **Work more** - Request overtime at work or get an additional job working part-time. If you are willing enough, there is work out there.

2. **Ask for a pay raise** - The best way to do this is present to your employer a compelling offer. Find out what frustrations or problems there are around your workplace and offer to solve them, and present this offer formally, along with your requested pay increase. Remember, the value of money is based on an agreement, so make a new agreement to increase your own value. You'll be surprised how effective this is. What have you got to lose?

3. **Find a better paying job** - If you don't get a pay raise, start looking for a better paying job elsewhere.

4. **Sell your junk -** This is a great way to quickly raise a bunch of cash. Clean out that room you have in your house where you keep all the junk. Collect all old electronic gadgets, TVs, etc., and sell the lot. You'll be amazed at how much cash you can raise by getting rid of things you really don't need. Not only is it a wonderful way to eliminate killer debt, it's also very liberating. You can allocate the income as usual, or add the lot to your Killer Allocation Account and hammer down that killer debt.

5. **Start a business part-time -** Start doing something you really enjoy and build up your income while working. You can start working for yourself and offer your services on sites like fiverr.com or upwork.com,

where people are looking for all kinds of help with editing, typing, design, programming and more. If you are interest, you can even start career as a Rich Habits Coach, creating additional income part-time and building your own business (see the chapter *Rich Habits Community and Coaching* for more details).

No matter what you do, you must approach your unviable situation with the same urgency as you would if you were drowning. You wouldn't sit down and watch TV if you were drowning, would you? So don't do it if you are drowning financially. Get viable immediately!

Get Viable Step 3 - Make More Money (Business)

If you own a business and have discovered that you are unviable, you must increase your profits and income. Here are two simple ways to do this:

1. **Increase your prices** - Start charging more for your products or services. A 10% increase in prices rarely gets noticed by customers; it's only the business owner who notices such things, yet 10% can make a significant difference to the overall profits. If you are going to put your prices up, however, you must ensure that you also improve your service in some way that doesn't cost money. This can be as simple as ensuring the product is delivered faster or adding something with a higher perceived value that costs you very little. And as a tip, don't tell your customers you have increased the price. Most of them won't even notice.

2. **Promote more** - To increase income, in a business, you need to sell more. To sell anything, you must promote.

Therefore the only expense you should <u>never</u> cut back on is advertising and promotion. You need to make sure your promotion is effective and actually bringing in clients and creating sales, but you should never skimp on promotion, because it's the only way out of financial difficulty for a business owner. (And for proven techniques on effective advertising and promotion, read my book *How to be a Marketing Genius* available at tonymelvin.com.)

Paying Too Much Tax

I have often run into people who do not want to increase their income for fear of paying more tax. As a consequence they waste a lot of time trying to avoid tax rather than increasing their income and getting more viable.

A friend of mine fell into this trap. As a high income earner he moved his family to the Bahamas, a tax haven, which has no income tax, no corporate tax, no capital gains tax, and no wealth tax. It's also a very lovely island situated in the Caribbean, with year round perfect weather. He spend a lot of time and money moving his business operation there. After 12 months or so, he realized the cost of living was so high that it was not worth the tax "saving." He and his family were also isolated from family and friends. He ended up returning to Australia. If he had focused his energies on making more money and paying the taxes, he would have been better off in the long run.

Therefore, when it comes to taxes, here's what you should do:

1. Make more money.

2. Seek legal and accounting advice to legally reduce tax simply.

3. Avoid complicated schemes that distract you from number 1.

If you need to make an extra $100,000 but you have to pay 30% tax, the easiest solution us to make $150,000. Better yet, aim for $300,000 and you'll have plenty left over.

— RICH HABIT —

The Rich focus primarily on making money and legally minimize tax when possible.

— POOR HABIT —

The Poor, in an effort to avoid tax, get distracted from making money.

Summary

If you are unviable, you need to apply the above and fix it fast. Once you have achieved True Viability, you must watch your viability graph closely and maintain it. And remember this Rich Habit.

— RICH HABIT —

The Rich are always viable.

— POOR HABIT —

The Poor tolerate being unviable.

12

ELIMINATING KILLER DEBT WITH THE SOLVENCY SYSTEM

If you have discovered you are insolvent or you have any form of killer debt, this chapter will start you on your journey up the Rich Continuum.

What you are about to read is not theory; it comes from hard-won experience. I developed this method while eliminating my killer debt. I call it the "Solvency System," and I have proven it is not a one-time fluke by successfully coaching others to implement it. Surprisingly, little has changed from when I first developed this method, except to make it easier to understand and to capitalize on certain changes in the law that helps speed up the process.

The most recent success of the Solvency System was with one gentleman I worked with, who was able to eliminate over $1.5 million of killer debt in 11 months, with less than $50,000. Here's an excerpt from an email he sent me:

Hi Tony,

I want to personally thank you for your time and expertise last year. I was in such a dark place and you helped me so much. I remember the feeling after I first met you. I said to myself that "everything is going to be fine".

From your book and your personal guidance and techniques, in the last 12 months I have negotiated (and settled) $1.571m in debt - on half my income.

I still have about $180K to go but the systems and processes have made it so much easier.

It's funny that most credit card companies, banks, loan companies, other debtors all operate with very similar systems. I have learnt to negotiate and hold my ground so many times now. As you taught me - no one has a gun to my head; no one can take money from my bank without my permission. My payments to them are on my terms.

In the last year, I have hit so many milestones:

1. Reduced my debt by 92%.
2. Reduced my monthly expenses by 48%.
3. Increased my income by 60%.
4. Settled all my tax debt.
5. Settled all my old business-related debt (over $800K).

But more importantly, I have reduced my stress; Increased my leisure time with my family and built a future with little debt and an increase in my income. I am now in control of my money rather than it controlling me.

The Solvency System is a 6-step process that will catapult you (or your business) up the Rich Continuum. It is a simple process and does not require any degrees or special skills. All that is required is your determination and a willingness to follow the system.

I want to point out that speed is not a measure of success. Your journey up the Rich Continuum is relative to you and no one else. Never compare your journey to another. And never undermine your progress. No matter how small your rise up the Rich Continuum, it is still better than before. I remember times at the beginning of my Rich Habits journey, all I managed to achieve was to prevent falling further down the Rich Continuum—that is still an accomplishment when swimming in the deep, so never abuse yourself or put yourself down. Nothing good will ever come from that. The rise up the Rich Continuum is more easily traveled when you congratulate yourself on every step you take, big or small.

Quite often, when paying past-due debts or bills, many use what I call the "Screaming System"—they simply pay the one who screams the loudest. This is not a very good system because you end up dealing with nothing but screaming creditors!

If you understand *who* you are dealing with, and if you understand a little of how the worldwide banking and financial system works, you can take control of your killer debt, stop the threatening phone calls and letters, negotiate the debt down and even in some cases, have the debt completely forgiven. You may be able to do all this without affecting your credit score.

A wonderful bonus of using the Solvency System is that it removes the stress, worry and anxiety associated with killer debt.

You'll be pleased to know, the Solvency System is included in the *Rich Habits Guidebook*, as an easy-to-follow checklist. Download it for free at myrichhabits.com.

Killer Debt Categories

First, let's identify the different categories of debt and *who* you owe money to, because each category below is handled a little differently.

These are the Killer Debt Categories; let's call them the KDC from now on:

1. **Family & Friends** - loans with family or friends.

2. **Small Business** - unpaid bills.

3. **Large Corporations** - unpaid bills.

4. **Banks & Credit Unions** - all types of loans including credit cards, store cards, personal loans, car leases, etc.

5. **Debt Collectors** - companies whose sole purpose is to collect money for unpaid bills or loans.

6. **Government** - unpaid taxes, parking fines and other fines.

7. **Lawsuits** - claims by another; an enforced payment of debts.

8. **Threatening or Potentially Violent Creditors** - people you owe money to who might resort to violence or force to get their money back.

The above list is a scale of sorts, with the top being the friendliest and easiest to deal with; as you move down the scale, the dealings become less friendly and more difficult. The level of unfriendliness and difficulty appears to parallel the amount of human involvement: the less human, the less friendly. It also parallels the amount of bureaucracy: the more rules and paperwork, the less friendly.

I recall having difficulty with KDCs 3, 4 and 6 until I was able to talk to someone who would listen and empathize. Therefore, this idea of the "Scale of friendliness" and the amount of human involvement is backed by actual experience. KDCs 7 and 8 rarely contain any friendliness whatsoever. Ironically, those in KDC 8 tend to come from the "friendly" KDC 1 and 2, but even they can be easily dealt with, when you know how.

The Solvency System

What you are about to learn works, if you follow it. It took me over 6 months before I paid a cent to any of my creditors, but all of them (those in KDCs 1, 2, 3 and 5) heard from me every week or so. I even got Christmas cards from some of them wishing me good luck for the New Year, despite not paying them a dime. This just goes to show the power of *communication* and *honesty*.

This method might appear too simple, but that doesn't reduce its effectiveness.

When crawling your way up from the bottom of the Rich Continuum, additional actions are required to ensure you survive while doing all that you can to make money.

If you happen to be a few weeks late on a mortgage payment or behind on rent, you are not in deep water, but these techniques will help you too.

Do the steps in this chapter at the same time as the "Get

Viable" steps in the previous chapter.

Ascending the Rich Continuum, from Poor, consists of these 6 steps:

1. Killer Debt List

2. Keep Accurate Records

3. Maintain a workable schedule

4. Killer Debt Communication and Control

5. Make Money and Allocate

6. Killer Debt Negotiation and Elimination

The essence of the Solvency System is to first bring the killer debt under control, while increasing your viability and Killer Debt Allocation, so you can be in a position to pay off or negotiate all killer debt. The following image illustrates the entire process.

Rich Habits Solvency System

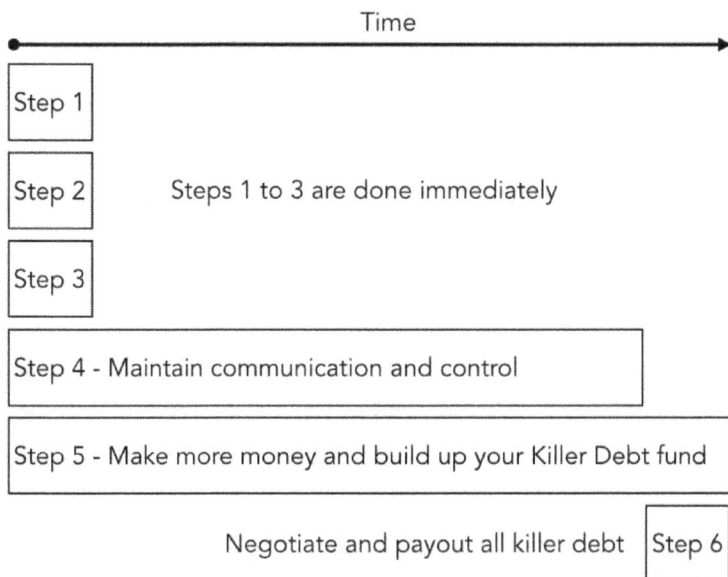

Time

Step 1

Step 2   Steps 1 to 3 are done immediately

Step 3

Step 4 - Maintain communication and control

Step 5 - Make more money and build up your Killer Debt fund

Negotiate and payout all killer debt   Step 6

Step 1: Killer Debt List

The first step is knowing exactly what is owed and who you owe it to. Remember the definition of "killer debt" and "assets" are:

— RICH HABITS DEFINITIONS —

Killer debt is money owed that is not backed by assets. It includes overdue or unpaid bills.

Assets are anything that has the potential to increase in value or provide an income and can be easily sold and converted to cash.

Make a list of all killer debt, who you owe it to, how much and include the category from the KDC list above. Be sure to put the full amount: even if you disagree with the amount at this stage, just put the full amount down (we will cover negotiating down your debt later).

Once you've done that, enter the due dates of each of the bills or debt.

Action Steps

1. Collect all the paperwork for all killer debt, including credit cards, loans, overdue bills, loans from family or friends. Record all the money you owe, that is not backed by assets, in every killer debt category.

2. Create a list (either handwritten or in a spreadsheet)

    2.1. Enter who is owed the money

    2.2. Enter the Killer Debt Category

    2.3 Enter the amount

    2.3. Enter the date the bill or debt was due.

3. Add up the total amount owed.

4. Enter the contact details of each creditor, phone, address, fax, email, etc.

5. Enter any special notes.

This is your Killer Debt List. I've provided an example for you below and a spreadsheet is included in the *Rich Habits Toolkit*, available for free from myrichhabits.com.

Killer Debt List

Creditor's Name	KDC	Contact Name	Amount Owed	Due Date	Phone	Fax	Email Address	Reference Number	Address	Notes
		Total								

Step 2: Keep Accurate Records

Getting out of debt has as much to do with paperwork as it does with money!

If you hate paperwork, you'll have to get over it. You must keep detailed records of all communication between you and your creditors. You are swimming with sharks, when in deep water, until you're solvent. And if you've got lawyers chasing you, that is no analogy!

The fact that I kept records of correspondence between myself and creditors saved my you-know-what several times. Because I was able to prove that I had sent several faxes to legal firms, I prevented them from taking me to court. If I hadn't kept a file, I would have had no proof and possibly lost despite all my prior efforts. So, I can't stress it enough, you need to keep written records.

If you are sending emails, be sure to print them out and file your hard copies; this will make it easy to find them, if needed. Backup your emails too. You can't be too careful about this.

The best way to do this is to file all correspondence under the creditor's name and keep it in date order. All the bills or invoices should be in the same folder too, with the paperwork for each creditor kept together with a binder clip. I call this the *Killer Debt File* and it makes it easy to find what you need.

I'll be honest, picking up my *Killer Debt File* was depressing, so I put a quote in big letters across the front to uplift my spirits. It went something like this:

You can simply realize it right now—you are untouchable and there is nothing that your creditors or anyone else can do to you. You can always fight back; you will always maintain your ability to create. You are unstoppable.

To be sure you do all your paperwork, and follow this Solvency System, you need a proper schedule.

Step 3: Maintain a Workable Schedule

To get out of deep water, it's good practice to organize your time effectively. In life, we all have many roles or hats we wear; for example, I have a father's hat, a husband's hat, a writer's hat, and when it comes to my businesses, a director's hat.

We all have to deal with money, so we all have to wear a "Rich Habits Hat." Some wear it well and others not so well, if at all! One of the reasons I got into such financial difficulty was because I didn't wear my Rich Habits Hat— basically I didn't do my job correctly as "Finance Manager," both personally and in my business.

When heading towards the goal of solvency, it's important to wear your Rich Habits hat, and wear it well. This means that you set aside the time specifically to carry out the actions explained in this book. Just like I make time for my Father Hat and Husband Hat, along with my other hats during the week, you need to make time for your Rich Habits Hat. That way, you'll actually do the steps we've covered so far!

Another very important reason for doing this is to avoid your creditors constantly bothering you. So that you can get on with the task of *making money,* notify your creditors of the best time to contact you. I made it every Friday afternoon between 1 p.m. and 4 p.m.. Actually, I made Friday afternoon and the evening my time to work on my communication to creditors, answering their calls or questions and doing my filing. By making this a habit, the creditors knew they could always reach me. Also, if a creditor happens to call at any other time, I'd say, "Friday is the day I take such calls because I'm busy on the job making money." You can also add that you don't have all the paperwork and particulars handy so Friday is better (or whatever time you choose).

My schedule during my journey up the Rich Continuum

Time	Monday	Tuesday	Wednesday	Thursday	Friday	Saturday	Sunday
8							
9					Working		
10							
11							
12						Working	
1	Working	Working	Working	Working			Working
2					Rich Habits Hat		
3							
4							
5					Working	Fun!	
6							

By doing it this way, you are in control of the situation and can, as I said, keep your mind focused on your job. But whatever you do, don't fail to wear the hat when you promise to do so. To avoid disappointing someone or forgetting to call them back, I would ask them to call me on Friday between 1 p.m. and 4 p.m.. I avoided promising them I would call them back, just in case I forgot. So don't feel bad about putting the onus back on them to call you. If they desperately want their money, they'll call.

By being organized in this way, you'll find that your creditors appreciate it. Anyone who balks at such a request will probably balk at anything you do, so don't worry about it, stick to your guns and communicate to all your creditors in one go—it makes the rest of the week enjoyable!

Control your schedule so you can focus on making

money and get solvent as soon as possible.

Step 4: Killer Debt Communicate and Control

Communication is so powerful and yet so under-utilized as a tool. Any conflict, from a lovers' tiff to a nation's war, is but a failure in communication.

When one fails to communicate, all manner of problems occur. Not paying a bill is a failure to communicate with your creditor using your money! Hence, if you cannot communicate with your money, you'd better communicate with something—otherwise the creditor loses faith in you. After all, payment was promised and the failure to fulfill that promise creates a problem for you and your creditor.

Let's assume you're in a relationship with another. If you stopped communicating with your partner or they stopped communicating with you, it's safe to assume the relationship would deteriorate. Also, if you started lying to your partner about something, this too would eventually deteriorate the relationship. Therefore, the quality of a relationship is directly proportional to the *quality* and *amount* of communication.

The same applies to any relationship, whether it's with your family, friends, coworkers, boss, employees, clients and yes, you guessed it—your creditors!

As soon as you realize you are not able to pay a bill or debt by the due date, you can save an enormous amount of trouble and stress by simply telling your creditor. Contact the person or company you owe money to and explain to them your situation and when you *will* pay. The majority of creditors are rather accommodating if you do this. Just think of all the time, effort and paperwork this would save the businesses of the world if people just called up and said, "Hi, I can't pay your bill on the due date, but I'll be able to pay it by the end of next month." The response is usually, "Okay, thanks for letting us know."

This is simply a matter of communication. But when you are in deep water it takes more than just a phone call to smooth things over. Your creditors probably know you're swimming at the bottom of the Rich Continuum because you haven't paid them for a while or you are always behind in your payments.

Therefore, this situation requires a very structured approach.

Before we discuss how you bring your killer debt under control, we first need to cover how to communicate to creditors.

Rich Habits Communication Rules

Here are the rules that worked for me, when communicating to creditors:

1. **Communicate.**

The more you communicate, the better. In the beginning, I was sending faxes to my KDC 1 to 4 creditors every week, no fail. Once I got control of things, I then sent a fax every month. Some creditors required more communication and whenever any legal proceeding commenced or when threatened, I'd communicate with the creditor even more.

2. **Be honest, tell the truth and never lie.**

Honesty is the best policy. Don't make it harder for yourself, just tell the truth.

3. **Only promise things you are 100% certain you can deliver.**

Never promise to pay money unless you already have it in the bank to pay. What you are trying to do with your communication is develop the creditor's trust in you. Anything that damages that trust will make it harder for you, so if in doubt, don't promise it. Remember that your word is your honor.

4. **Keep it positive.**

Always talk about the good things you are doing. Thank them for their patience. Tell them about your plans and future goals. By keeping them informed in this way, they become more confident about you and your ability to pay. Never blame anyone else for your debt (even if it is true). A creditor doesn't care *why* you got into debt; all they care about is how they are going to get paid. So stick to the positive and you'll win.

These 4 simple rules are what got me out of debt unscarred. They could be called the "Golden Rules"—and when you think about it, they apply to life in general.

There are some additional rules when communicating with your creditor that you should follow:

5. **Always put your communication in writing.**

This can be a letter, fax or email. Any phone call or meeting should be documented immediately with any agreements made duly noted and sent in writing to all concerned. Even if it was a simple discussion, a record of it should be made and sent to all parties. It could be as simple as: *"Hi Joe, thanks for the call today. Still working on the job! Appreciate your patience on this matter. Regards …."*

6. **Include the date.**

This is so you can keep accurate records.

7. **Include reference numbers.**

Include invoice numbers, account numbers, or possibly a legal reference number. That way, the recipient can easily file it and it doesn't get lost! You want to ensure your communication is received by the person or people you send it to, so make sure all the details are there so it is easy for them to file.

8. **Include all your contact details.**

This includes your phone numbers, fax number, address and email. Not only does this make it easy for people to contact you, it also shows that you are not hiding or running away. Knowing that they can contact you is another factor that increases the creditor's confidence and trust in you.

Every letter or email you send must follow these guidelines. Here is an example of mine:

[Date]

[Credit's Company Name]
[Company Address]
[Company Phone]
[Company Fax]

Attention: **[Contact Name]**
Your Reference: **[Reference Number]**

Dear [Contact Name],

I'd like to take this opportunity to update you on my current situation.

As a means to ensure all my creditors are paid back the money owed, I have searched out a viable way to provide substantial income.

As of two weeks ago, I secured a marketing role with a property development group in Sydney that pays me a regular weekly income of $500. In addition to that I'm paid on a reward basis for property sales at a rate of $4,000 per property sold personally and slightly lower commission for sales generated through my marketing methods.

The hours for this role are somewhat flexible with weekends and mornings free. This provides me with the ability to earn additional income through the cleaning business I have also started.

With all of this income generating activity, I am confident to be able to maintain regular monthly payments. When commissions from property sales are received, I'll be able to contribute larger sums.

I trust this is an acceptable arrangement. Of course, I can appreciate that this debt has been outstanding for quite a while, however, I hope you see that my efforts are sincere.

Regards,

Tony Melvin

[Address]
[Mobile Number] [Work Number]
[Home Number]
[Email Address]

An editable copy is available in the *Rich Habits Toolkit*

Keep in mind that I was really in the deep and had, at that time, recently secured regular income. Therefore, I wrote about my efforts of getting viable and the kind of money I was able to earn to give them *hope* that I was going to make enough to pay off the debt.

Killer Debt Control

These are the steps you take to get each of these KDCs under immediate control.

KDC 1 Control - Family and Friends

Communicate the situation to your family or friend whom you owe money. You might want to do this in person or over the phone. I strongly suggest you follow up any personal or phone contact in writing (email or letter). In fact, to ensure all points are fully explained, you might want to write a letter and get them to read it first, then answer any questions they may have. Remember the Communication Rules above, especially #3. Never promise payment. The only promise you should make is to keep them informed of your progress.

This is usually all it takes to bring KDC 1 under control. If discussions get heated or they start making unrealistic demands and threaten to sue you, handle them as you would a KDC 7. If they threaten violence in any way handle them as a KDC 8.

KDC 2 Control - Small Business

Send a written explanation of your situation, following the Communication Rules. Always offer to talk and answer questions. This is usually all it takes to bring this killer debt under control.

KDC 3 Control - Large Corporations

While large companies often appear impersonal and overwhelming, never forget they are made up of human beings! There is someone responsible for your loan or bill. Often, large companies are caught up in the red tape and lose their sense of compassion, but only a human being can have compassion and understanding—no amount of company policies or procedures can create it.

When communicating to anyone, still follow the 8 Communication Rules mentioned. Often, the communication is verbal, via the phone or over the counter. In this case, get the name and email address of the person you spoke to so you can send a written follow-up message afterwards, if only for your own records.

There are two methods of controlling this killer debt. One is the proactive approach used before the bill is due; the other is when the bill is already overdue. The one you use depends on where you sit on the Rich Continuum.

Proactive Extension

If you know you cannot pay a bill by the due date, be proactive, call them up and ask for an extension. Keep in mind, some companies will not provide an extension until after the due date. In that case, ask that a note be made on your file and set a reminder to call them back after the due date to request an extension.

Overdue Bill Extension

Contact the company and ask for an extension of 3

months. They might not give you that long, but try. If the person is unwilling or unable to grant an extension, you might need to talk with a different department. Most large companies have a Hardship Department, so ask for that. If they don't have a Hardship Department, politely hang up and try again. Usually, it takes no more than three attempts to get someone who is willing to help you.

KDC 4 Control - Banks and Credit Unions

You have two options to bring credit cards, personal loan, and leases under control. Keep in mind, in the case of credit cards, both of these options assume that you will cease using them immediately. Only unviable people need to borrow to live— it's a poor habit.

Option 1 - On Hold - Credit cards can be put on hold for 3 months, with no fees, no interest and no penalties. Personal loans can be "paused" with little or no interest or payment required for 3 months, as can home loans. To make these arrangements, simply call the company and ask for the Hardship Department. Always ask for 6 months and they'll give you 3. Also, this grace period usually has no effect on your credit score, but be sure to ask and get confirmation. Most banks will send written confirmation of the arrangement, but follow the Communication Rules and get the details of the person you spoke with and keep a record of it.

This arrangement can usually be repeated a total of two times, giving you roughly 6 months' grace period; after that, if not paid, the debt is passed onto debt collectors.

Option 2 - The KD Shuffle - The whole purpose is to "shuffle" your loans to reduce or eliminate interest charges. This is mostly easily done with credit cards. You apply for a new card and transfer the balance of the old one to the new one, which will have a zero or very low rate of interest for the first 6-18 months. Every dollar paid towards the card is now reducing your killer debt, moving you up the Rich Continuum.

Depending on your situation, you might utilize Option 1 for the first 6 months and then use Option 2 paying everything off without any interest. Or, if you have lots of killer debt, after using Option 1, you might want to negotiate the debt for a reduced amount. We'll cover how that's done in Step 6 of the Solvency System, but with the above methods, your KDC 4 is now under control.

KDC 5 Control - Debt Collectors

Debt collectors are interested in only one thing: collecting money (surprise!). As such, they are not interested in granting extensions. Debt collectors make money in one of two ways, they either 1) get a percentage of what they collect or 2) buy the debt from the company you owed money to at a reduced rate (as low as 10% of the debt or less) and then try to collect the full amount from you. For example, if you owe a company $10,000, the debt collector might pay $1,000; now he wants to get $10,000 from you, so he can make a $9,000 profit.

To bring the debt under control, you can either jump straight to the negotiations as covered in Solvency Step 6 or you can contact the original company you owed the money to, and apply KDC 3 control method. This worked for me, by the way; I'll explain the story in more detail later, but as a quick summary; I had a legal firm chasing and threatening me with legal action unless I paid today (remember the phone call from *Harass & Partners?*). Well, that lead me to contacting the company directly, and the head of the finance department fired the legal firm and told them to leave me alone. So, I moved that killer debt from a KDC 5 back to KDC 3 and under my control.

KDC 6 Control - Government

This category works similar to a KDC 3, so the same methods apply. Ask for an extension of 3 to 6 months, without fees, penalties or payments. You can do this several times. Keep in mind, if you don't get someone willing to help you, politely hang up and call back.

KDC 7 Control - Lawsuits

To bring this one under control, you will probably need to get legal advice and employ a lawyer to act on your behalf. But if you were as poor as I was, you might not even be able to afford a lawyer. My approach was the same as KDC 3, only all communication was in writing. My experience with *Harass & Partners* taught me the value of communicating directly to the company I owed money to, and this stopped all legal actions in all cases except one; therefore, you can move a KDC 7 back to KDC 3 with communication.

KDC 8 Control - Threatening or Potentially Violent Creditors

If someone threatens you to "pay up or else!" and are implying physical harm to you or your family, this is called "extortion." It is *a crime of obtaining something such as money or information from somebody by using force, threats, or other unacceptable methods*. Extortion is illegal in most countries. A person does not necessarily need to actually do anything to you—the mere act of threatening you is extortion.

If any creditor threatens you or implies in any way that "there will be consequences if you don't pay now," then quote the above paragraph and report them to the police immediately.

I'm not kidding. Don't take it lightly. You can contact the police and make a statement. This becomes a matter of police record. The police won't take any action other than to take your statement and make it a matter of record. You normally receive a Police Record Number.

I was threatened in this way and immediately reported it. I then sent my creditor an email with the police record number and my interpretation of the incident. I stated that if anything happened to me, or my family, I had instructed several of my friends to immediately report the incident to the police with reference to that record number. He backed away completely and patiently waited for his money. So don't be afraid of creditors like this; the law is there to back you up.

I still applied the Communication Rules, and with the method above, I moved this debt back to a KDC 1 and under control. As soon as I was able to (some 12 months after the threat), I got a personal loan and paid him in full. He later apologized for his actions.

Summary of Step 4

Applying these methods above brings the killer debt under <u>your</u> control. These steps immediately improve your viability, as this debt is now on hold, without any monthly payments required. The next step is to make more money.

Step 5: Make Money and Allocate

This step is self-explanatory. You have to make money to get out of deep water and get solvent.

These are a summary of the ideas provided in the prior chapter:

1. Request overtime at work or get an additional job working part-time.

2. Ask for a pay raise.

3. Find a better paying job.

4. Sell your junk via yard sale, Craigslist or eBay.

5. Start a business or sell your services via fiverr.com or upwork.com.

You also need to build up the funds in your Killer Debt Allocation account, as this will be needed for the Killer Debt Negotiation step. The key to building up your Killer Debt Allocation account is to start following the Laws of Allocation and implementing the first two fundamental Rich Habits:

1. The rich *always* **allocate**.

2. The Rich are *always* **viable**.

Step 6: Killer Debt Negotiation and Elimination

The Rich habit that applies to this step is:

— RICH HABIT —

The Rich know everything is negotiable.

— POOR HABIT —

The Poor compromise.

The Rich know everything is negotiable, even killer debt. The Poor rarely negotiate. Instead, they comprise, which in this sense means *the acceptance of standards that are lower than is desirable.* Paying more than 20% interest on a credit card is a compromise, especially when it's possible to remove all interest payments and even pay out the entire debt with only 10%.

My Negotiation Story

During my period of insolvency, I was working two different businesses. One provided regular income so that I was viable; the other was in property development which would provide the bigger commissions needed to pay off $300,000 of killer debt.

The problem with property development was I had to wait anywhere from 6 to 18 months before I received any money. However, when these property deals were paid for, I received a large lump sum. Whenever I received such a sum, I wrote a letter to each creditor offering between

10% to 50% of the debt as full and final payment.

When I first did this, I was able to eliminate over $80,000 of debt with about $35,000. That was a good week!

Some creditors refused, so I maintained my communication with them.

About half actually took this option when I offered it, and I still deal with several of those businesses today. Because they helped me when I needed it, there is a loyal business relationship that is not based on price, but on trust and friendship. And since that time, I have not only spent thousands of dollars with them, but have referred plenty of business to them too. Their kind gesture to me has been repaid, in full, several times over.

Reduced payment is an option that many creditors will accept. When you consider that debt collectors cost money and a bankrupt person rarely pays anything, a reduced payment is a fair option from someone who could declare bankruptcy. Of course, you don't threaten your creditors into accepting a reduced payment; if a creditor is able and happy to wait for the full amount, that is fair for both parties too.

Negotiation Methods

The two factors that determine the type of negotiation tactic you use are: 1) the KDC you are dealing with and 2) your position on the Rich Continuum.

The lower you are on the Rich Continuum, the more you will want to negotiate the debt down. If you are just under broke, you might not need to negotiate; you simply need to get it under control and continue applying the Rich Habits until it is paid off in full.

KDC 1 Negotiation - Family and Friends

Most people prefer to repay family and friends in full, and thankfully, family and friends are usually accommodating and rarely employ debt collectors or take legal action. If there is little or no interest being charged, then extended terms won't affect your solvency. The negotiation tactic is the same as the control method outlined in Step 4: let them know what is happening and tell them you'll repay the amount when you have made the money. Really, all you need is more time, and that is your focus in negotiations with this KDC. If, however, it turns nasty and they do resort to debt collectors (KDC 5) or take legal action against you (KDC 7), then apply the tactics outlined for those types of KDCs.

KDC 2 Negotiation - Small Business

Small business owners are usually very easy to deal with. Applying the process outlined in Step 4 is often enough to keep them satisfied. They are also quite open to a settlement of the debt at reduced rate, once you have built up cash in your Killer Debt Allocation account.

About 30% of my killer debt fell into this KDC and most of it was settled for around 50% of the actual amount, and I still deal with these businesses today.

KDC 3 Negotiation - Large Corporations

Now we're moving into less friendly territory for the simple fact that we are dealing more with bureaucracy (rules and paperwork). The collection departments of large corporations operate on fixed policies and predetermined systems. If you don't pay a bill on time you automatically get a reminder letter, each subsequent letter is more threatening and after 30 or 60 days, your "file" is sent to a debt collector. The communications method recommended in Step 4 can delay this process, providing you with more time to pay. However, if you are below Rich -10.0, you might not be able to pay at all. In this case, you may have to deal with the debt collectors (KDC 7).

But despite large corporations appearing soulless, the individuals who work there aren't, and it is possible to negotiate a reduced payout of the debt. The trick is to make sure you are talking to the right department. Ask if they have a Hardship Department; if so, you can often negotiate up to 50% of the total debt, or perhaps remove all late fees, etc. Never be afraid to ask. If they say no you haven't lost anything, and they might just accept. The key to negotiating is to have the money ready to pay immediately; you are making the offer and can do it today.

KDC 4 Negotiation - Banks and Credit Unions

You should already have your credit cards and loans on hold or transferred the balance to an interest-free loan. Once you have enough in your Killer Debt Allocation account, you are ready for negotiations.

All banks have a hardship department, so ensure you are communicating directly to that department. Sometimes, banks employ a legal firm to handle negotiations.

When dealing directly with the banks (and not their debt collectors), you can negotiate up to 50% of the actual debt, as a final payout. Negotiation is usually a back-and-forth process. You offer a payout of 10% and they'll counter your offer with 80%. Stick to your 10%, and they'll slowly come down to around 50%. This may take 3 months by the way. Don't fret it; at this stage, it's not adversely affecting your solvency.

If your debt has been passed onto a debt collector, then the process is slightly different.

KDC 5 Negotiation - Debt Collectors

Debt collectors have only one weapon. It's the only tool they know how to use and they use it every single time, in every single communication—they try to intimidate you.

They intimidate you by threatening legal action, with late fees, with a bad credit score—each intimidation is like a sword they poke and prod you with. It's extremely alarming, upsetting and stressful. As such, you dread the phone calls and the letters. Every time the phone rings, you wonder if it's a debt collector. Opening the mail makes your stomach do summersaults.

Here's the good news: That sword they poke and prod you with, is not a sword at all. It's a toothpick and it's blunt. A debt collector can do nothing to you, especially when you know how the game works.

As mentioned in Step 4, debt collectors make their money by: 1) as "Fee Collector" charging a percentage of money collected or 2) as a "Debt Buyer" where they acquire your debt from the company at a reduced rate.

If you have a Fee Collector chasing you for money, by communicating directly to the company you actually owe money to (as in Step 4 control for KDC 2 and 3), you will often find that the Fee Collector (the debt collector) is taken out of the picture.

However, if the debt collector is a "Debt Buyer," then the original company will no longer be responsive to your communications and you are stuck with dealing directly with the debt collector. This is great news however because you know that the debt collector has purchased your debt at a discount, and you know you can negotiate. Start by offering 10% of the debt as full and final payment. Now, when you do this, you will receive, as a reply, the only tool they know how to use. They will try to intimidate you will legal action, with late fees, with a bad credit score —just picture them thrusting a blunt toothpick at you. When they realize you cannot be intimidated, they'll put away the toothpick and start negotiating. Often this takes several phone calls; they'll call, threaten you with a deadline, and when the deadline passes and nothing happens, they'll call again. Eventually, they'll stop the intimidation and start talking numbers.

I recall a phone call I received from a debt collector who started the phone call saying that I was lucky he got hold of me today, because this debt needed to be paid today and if I didn't pay, I was going to be in big trouble and possibly go to jail. The amount I owed was about $300, and it was from a utility company of a prior residence where I lived, I never received the final bill because it was sent to the old residence. I was fully solvent by this time and sitting comfortably at the top of the Rich

Continuum. Anyhow, I listened to this guy rant and threaten me, while at the same time pretending to be my friend. Once he was done, I asked him to send me a copy of the actual bill and I'd pay it directly to the utility company. He tried to intimidate me again and I repeated my requests, unfazed by his threats (no one is ever going to jail for $300!). By the end of the call, he was begging me to pay directly via him rather than directly to the utility company as it would help his "business." I think I broke his toothpick.

In summary, don't feel intimidated; they can't do anything to you. They don't hold a gun to your head. You can hold your ground and negotiate.

KDC 6 Negotiation - Government

Many countries around the world have a hardship program for tax debt whereby the entire tax debt can be forgiven. It usually requires special circumstances of hardship. It is really reserved for those down at the bottom of the Rich Continuum and for those who have suddenly found themselves in financial difficulty because of the loss of a loved one or a natural disaster. Regardless, I always encourage people to apply for debt forgiveness; at the very least, it buys you more time!

If debt forgiveness is rejected, the next option is to negotiate a payment plan that you *know for sure* you can stick to. I suggest you set up a specific allocation for this amount, with its own bank account and put the money aside from every paycheck as part of your unusable income. That means you remove it from your income *before* you do any further allocations.

To give you an idea of what is possible, when I was in my difficult situation, I had a tax debt of about $50,000. I managed to negotiate a 2-year payment plan with all fees and interest removed—that saved me over $15,000. I was paying about $500 per month with a lump sum payment at the end of two years. It took 4 attempts to negotiate this because I was told that $500 per month was not enough. But I kept trying because *everything is negotiable!*

KDC 7 Negotiation - Lawsuits

Ironically, there is a tremendous benefit to being down in the deep, swimming with the sharks, at the bottom of the Rich Continuum. It's this: they can't make you poorer!

Whenever I was threatened by a debt collector or legal firm, whereby they would mention bankruptcy or taking me to court, my reply was always, "Great, you'd be doing me a favor."

My viewpoint was simple: *I'm trying to make good, I'm working hard and my intention is to pay back the debt; I could easily declare bankruptcy but I'm trying to avoid that. If you want to push me over the edge, then you'll get nothing. But if you give me a chance, you will get something. It's your call.*

You see, I realized that I had nothing to lose. I'd already lost it. *So, what can they really do? Sure, bankruptcy would be a pain, and create hurdles down the road, but in reality, it won't stop me.* That attitude prevented any legal action. It also stopped all such threats.

You are, in truth, invincible. They can take your house, and they can make you bankrupt, but they'll never, ever take your ability to create and start anew. There's only one person in the world who can prevent you from rising back up the Rich Continuum, and that's you. You are unstoppable.

This attitude should not be discounted or passed off as a cliché pep talk. To make the point, one gentleman I helped was in $300,000 of credit card and tax debt, plus he was being personally sued for over a million dollars by his ex-business partners. After getting clarity on the Rich Habits and applying the Solvency System, he had the tax debt and credit cards under control. In a clearer frame of mind and a huge change in attitude, he read through the lawsuit and discovered a blaring obvious error. The firm that was suing him had already accepted $20,000 as compensation that they were now trying to get $1 million for. So, a quick letter outlining this point, with an offer of $5,000 to go away and the deal was settled. He told me he never would have even noticed this, had it not been for the fact that he was no longer stressed about his finances. Prior to that, he was trying to negotiate his way of out of the lawsuit and avoid it.

But, if it does turn into a legal battle, then get your own lawyers and let them deal with it. And don't be afraid to fight.

KDC 8 Negotiation - Threatening or Potentially Violent Creditors

You should have handled these people as part of Solvency Step 4 and moved them back into a KDC 1. If you want to negotiate a reduced amount with them, you might want to do so via a lawyer. I certainly wouldn't meet them in person alone; take somebody with you, like Dwayne Johnson or your mother-in-law, whoever is the scariest. Kidding aside, even if they have backed down, any negotiation attempts might get heated, so be sensible and take precautions. Preferably, do all negotiation in writing, from a distance and start low.

Legal and Accounting Firms

As an alternative to personally handling Killer Debt Negotiations yourself, you can use a legal firm to act on your behalf, for KDCs 4 & 5. For Tax debts (KDC 6) you can ask your accountant to handle the negotiations. This is a great way to take the pressure off yourself so you can focus on making money and getting solvent. Also, I think when debt collectors deal with lawyers, they knock off all intimidation attempts and simply get down to negotiation. And your accountant is used to dealing with the tax office.

I know one circumstance where $120,000 of credit card debt was negotiated down to less than $20,000, using a legal firm whose fees totaled $5,000, so the legal cost covered themselves in saved time and money.

Using Your Killer Debt Fund

As mentioned earlier, your killer debt funds are specifically for paying off killer debt. For all methods mentioned above, pay out the debt using the funds in your Killer Debt Allocation account.

If you don't have enough money in your Killer Debt Allocation account, you need to earn more or allocate more of your income towards killer debt. At one point, I was setting aside 50% of my income, as well as most of my bonus income, to speed up the process of getting solvent.

Credit Score

One of the biggest tricks played on our current society is the need for a "good credit score." If Poor Habits are a plague, then the credit score is the virus.

One of the most common questions I receive in relation to applying the Solvency System is: "How will this affect my credit score?"

For people very insolvent, below Rich level -10.0, often their score has already been affected, especially if their debt has been passed onto debt collectors. Applying the Solvency System will usually not make it any worse. But regardless, my response to this is, "So what? What happens if you have a bad credit score?"

"I can't get a loan!" they'll exclaim.

"Perfect," I reply.

They look at me shocked and puzzled. So I explain it further, "Then you'll be *forced* to apply the Rich Habits. You have to be viable, you'll have to be solvent, and you won't be able to spend money you don't have. Sounds perfect to me."

Often, they are worried about getting a home loan or a car loan in the future. But, no matter how bad your credit score is, you can always improve it later, and when you practice Rich Habits, your credit score naturally improves.

Remember this Rich Habit:

— RICH HABIT —

The Rich use debt to invest (Investment debt).

— POOR HABIT —

The Poor use debt to spend (Killer debt).

A bad credit score is the best thing that can happen to a person practicing Poor Habits, because it prevents them from accumulating more killer debt.

Summary of the Solvency System

Now you know the Rich Habits Solvency System. Armed with this knowledge, you can start your journey up the Rich Continuum. The next chapter provides more information for those close to bankruptcy and those with a company that is in real financial difficulty, for there is still light at the end of that deep, dark tunnel.

13

The Legal Game

If you find yourself in a situation where you are forced into bankruptcy, despite all efforts to avoid it, it's worth understanding what it is and how it works so you can survive the process with as few scars as possible.

Bankruptcy

The word "bankrupt" comes from the Italian word *banca rotta*. "Banca" means *bench or table* and refers to the type of counter used in money lending shops around 1530 and "rotta" means *broken*; so the word used to mean *broken table* implying that when the money lender's bench broke, they were out of business!

Today, the word "bankrupt" in the financial sense means *the inability to pay one's debts*. It applies to the individual, and the intention of bankruptcy laws are to stop the bankrupt person from wasting what wealth they have left. A person's assets can be seized and sold, with the proceeds paid proportionately to each creditor based on the amount they are owed. Bankruptcy also serves as a way for a person to start afresh, free from the burden of overwhelming debt.

When a person is made bankrupt and their assets sold, there are usually certain restrictions or penalties the person must endure. Often, it's very difficult to borrow money for a period of time. It is also possible for the law to enforce payment to creditors from future income. In addition to such penalties is the stigma of being made bankrupt.

Despite its drawbacks, bankruptcy is a valid method of jumping up the Rich Continuum back to Broke, if the killer debt has gotten out of control and attempts at debt negotiation prove fruitless. Think of it as a way to "reset" your position back to the middle. Depending on your situation, it might be the simplest solution for you.

Keep in mind, the law has provisions for "repeat offenders" who use bankruptcy as a reset too many times, and unethical conduct is not ignored; nevertheless, if you decide to hit the "reset button," remember to start afresh with Rich Habits and your journey will be much smoother.

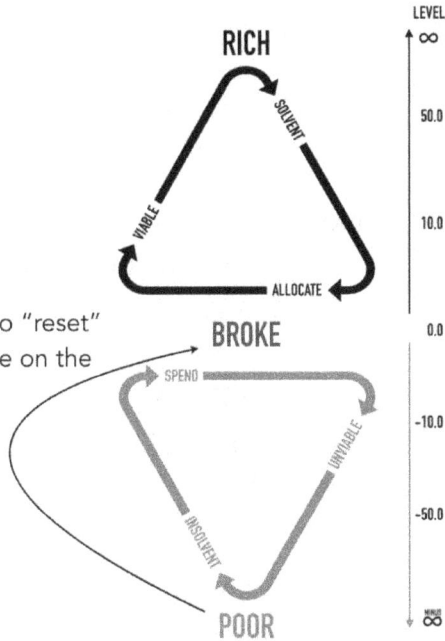

Bankruptcy

Bankruptcy is a way to "reset" your position to Broke on the Rich Continuum and eliminate all debt, but it has some strings attached.

Administration and Liquidation

While bankruptcy is a legal option for individuals, corporations (when insolvent) use an entirely different process called Administration. It such an instance, creditors can appoint an administrator who is responsible for improving the business and making it solvent. An administrator replaces the current directors on a temporary basis until the company is "rescued." If the administrator cannot improve the business, the next option is liquidation in which all the assets of the business are sold and the profits distributed evenly among the creditors based on the amount owed to them.

Unlike bankruptcy, where an individual's records are tarnished for several years, company directors can walk away unscathed from a liquidation process; however, it does depend on the circumstances. Should an investigation reveal illegal activities by those in power, they can suffer a much worse fate.

Just as bankruptcy is a "reset" for the individual, liquidation acts as a reset whereby the company directors are free to start again from scratch. But, it can often be avoid. I have helped many business on the verge of collapse jump back up the Rich Continuum, avoiding administration and liquidation. If you want help in this area see the chapter *Rich Habits Community & Coaching*.

Liquidation

Liquidation is a way to "reset" a business entity back to Broke on the Rich Continuum, allowing the business owners to start again, from scratch. It too has certain restrictions.

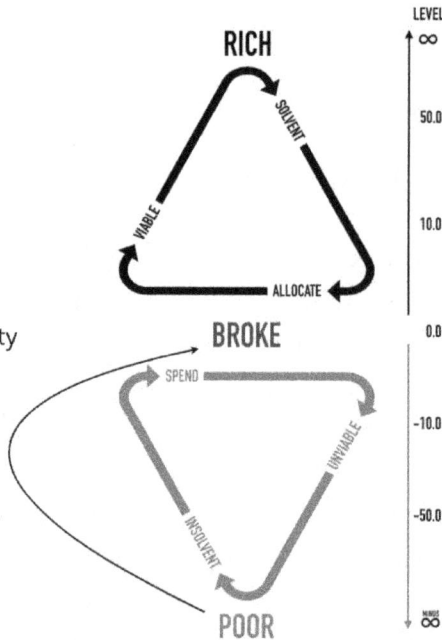

The System Flaw

There are instances whereby, given enough time, a person can rise up the Rich Continuum and avoid bankruptcy or salvage their business and repay all debts, however despite these efforts the individual may find themselves swamped with legal battles, and either through pure frustration, or stress, or exhausted resources, decides to throw in the towel and hits "reset."

I know what it's like because it almost happened to me. The fault here is not with the individual, but with the legal system and from my experience the system is somewhat flawed.

Remember the company *Harass & Partners* I mentioned in the beginning of the book? I was extremely puzzled at the time as to why they would pursue bankruptcy when I had made it very clear that I owned nothing and was in a lot of debt.

Pictures help me think clearer, so I decided to draw who was involved in this situation to figure out what benefit *Harass & Partners* hope to gain by enforcing bankruptcy.

By drawing the following pictures, I realized that *Harass & Partners* only get paid when chasing me for money. They get very little if I pay the debt back. Then it dawned on me: they get paid by their client regardless of whether I pay the bill or not and by issuing proceedings against me they were able to bill their client more time—time for every letter, every phone call, every fax! The more paperwork they could create, the more they got paid; it had very little to do with collecting the debt.

Because I owed such a little amount (only $3,575), the amount the legal firm was set to make (if I paid the debt in full) was probably a lot less than the fees involved in pursuing matter. Then it occurred to me: *this whole system is rigged to make you go bankrupt or to at least encourage it.* In other words, if you're working your darnedest to really pay off your debts, that doesn't serve the lawyers; it may serve your creditor in the end or the person you owe money to, but it doesn't actually serve the legal system.

Step 1

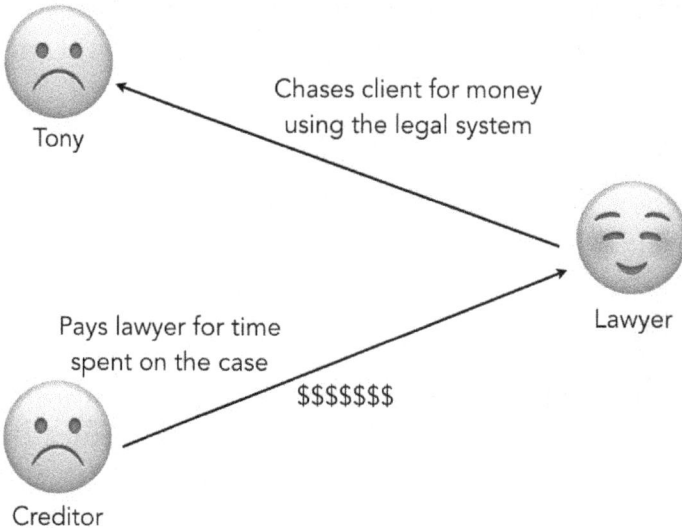

Tony

Chases client for money using the legal system

Lawyer

Pays lawyer for time spent on the case

$$$$$$$

Creditor

Step 2

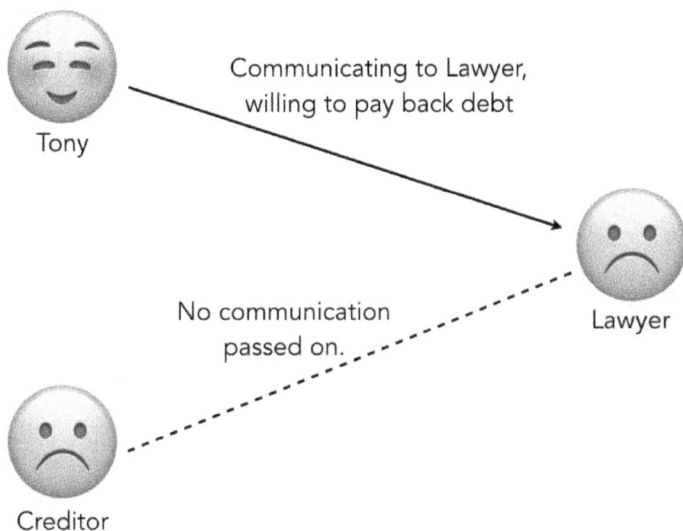

Tony

Communicating to Lawyer,
willing to pay back debt

Lawyer

No communication
passed on.

Creditor

Step 3

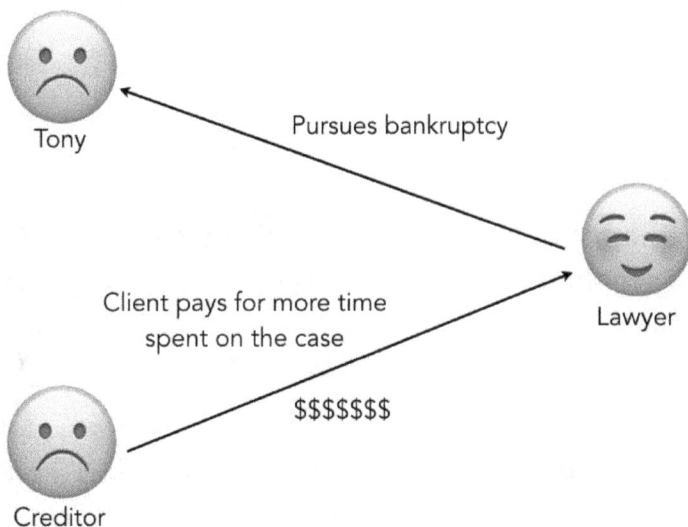

Tony

Pursues bankruptcy

Lawyer

Client pays for more time
spent on the case

$$$$$$$

Creditor

The legal system, as a bureaucracy, makes its money by

more paperwork: more filing, more phoning, more faxes and more time. Realizing this, I thought, "Well, I'm going to bypass the lawyer and send my letters directly to the creditors."

Step 4

Tony

Communicates directly to creditor explaining situation and intentions

Lawyer

Creditor

After that phone call I received from *Harass & Partners*, later that night I went back to the office and gathered a copy of all the letters I had sent to their office. I then wrote the following letter to the head of Company X Credit Department.

I repeated this process for all of the other creditors where I had been corresponding directly with a legal firm, rather than with the actual creditor. The result was amazing.

[Date]
[Company Name]
[Company Address]
[Company Phone] ,[Company Fax]

Attention: **[Contact Name]**
Your Reference: **[Reference Number]**

Dear [Contact Name],

This fax is in response to the telephone conversation I had with Sol Licit today from your legal firm Harass & Partners. I was informed that bankruptcy proceedings will commence unless I pay in full immediately.

I would like to point out that I'm very surprised that legal proceedings have developed this far when my intentions have been clearly outlined all along. However, I can understand that without any money being paid, one is prone to conclude that these words and the efforts behind them bear no real substance and are worthless.

Yet the idea of enforcing bankruptcy, from my understanding, has no real benefit for either party. The creditor receives a portion of the funds and the debtor's record is tarnished. It seems the only real winner is the legal eagles who get paid no matter what. It seems like a fruitless endeavor when you consider that I have no assets or wealth of any kind. If I did, I would sell them and pay off the debt! The only way I'll be able to pay back the money is through sweat and blood which is what I'm doing.

Before any further action is taken, I'd like to ensure you have received all of my communications. You should have received the following written faxes from me:

1. Faxed [date]
2. Faxed [date]
3. Faxed [date]
4. Faxed [date] (attached)

All of these clearly outline my efforts along with updates on my address changes and contact numbers. I can send copies of all my faxes if you wish.

I intend to pay the debt. I am not going anywhere; I'm simply working hard to handle this situation. I've included my details below. If you have any questions, please call.

I hope you can see my intentions are honest and sincere.

Regards,

Tony Melvin

On Monday morning I received an unexpected call from the head of finance at Company X. He said, "Tony, I've got your fax and we were totally unaware of this so thank you very much for sending them to me. I also want you to know that it's obvious, to me, that you're trying your best and that you will more than likely pay this amount off. So I've called off the dogs. You pay when you've got the money."

I said, "Thanks very much for that, I really appreciate it, would you mind putting that in writing?" Which he was more than willing to do. I got similar phone calls or replies back from all the other creditors who were using legal firms. They all said something along these lines, "We understand you don't have the money and you're obviously trying to make good, so keep in touch and let us know how you're going."

But the interesting part to this is that the lawyer from *Harass & Partners* still tried to pursue the legal bankruptcy and I continued to get letters and phone calls from them for several months. I wrote a letter to them asking them to cease these ridiculous and petty practices and copied it to my "friend" at Company X. He called me saying, "I don't know what these guys are doing because I'm not paying them for this. They seem to be off on their own little tangent. Don't worry, we won't follow through with it." I knew if Company X wasn't going to follow through, the lawyers really had no leg to stand on.

Harass & Partners were obviously trying to squeeze as much money as they could from this situation and failed. That was one of those moments you cherish, those moments when you know exactly what someone is trying to do to you and you've beaten them at their own game. That was pure pleasure and I never heard from them again.

Step 5

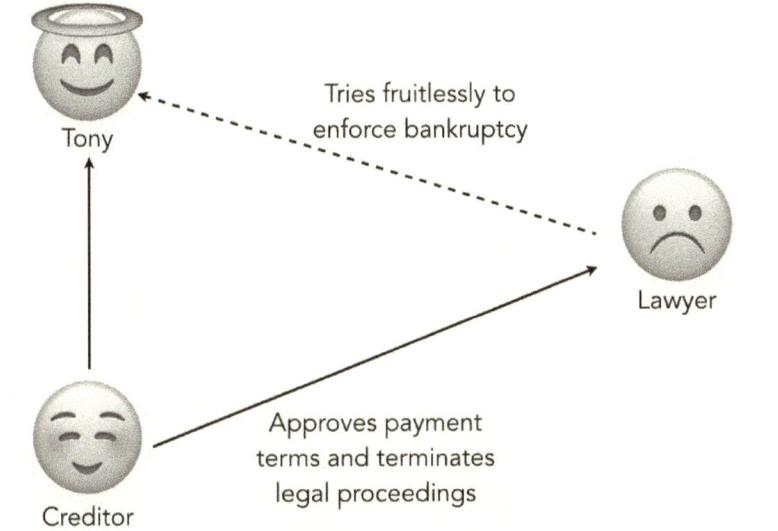

Tony — Tries fruitlessly to enforce bankruptcy — Lawyer

Creditor — Approves payment terms and terminates legal proceedings

I'd like to point out that not all legal firms are like this (yes, I've heard all the lawyer jokes too!). Only four of the companies I owed money to used legal firms and *Harass & Partners* was the only one who acted in this way.

The lesson learned is this: *Always communicate directly to those you owe money to and do it in writing.*

But despite the depressing nature of this chapter, remember this: all of these unfortunate circumstances can easily be avoided if one knows and follows the Rich Habits.

14

FRIEND OR FOE

There is one more skill that is paramount to your future success. Without it, you will run into difficulty and your journey up the Rich Continuum will be hindered, even if you learn and apply the Rich Habits.

The skill is being able to tell the difference between a *friend* and a *foe*.

Let's define these terms.

A "foe" is *an enemy or opponent*. It comes from an Old English word *fāh*, which means *hostile* and is the same origin of the word *feud*, which means *to quarrel, conflict*.

A "friend" is *a person who is not an enemy, a person who is on the same side*. It comes from the Germanic word *freund* which means *to love*, and is the same origin of the word *free*.

Many years ago, I had a business idea to build a national accounting firm in Australia. I thought the industry was perfect. It had repeat customers who were required *by law* to come back again the following year; every business needs an accountant; and I could see the industry was ripe for some clever marketing and efficiencies.

So I started looking for an accounting firm I could partner with and build into a large, national practice.

I met with many but none had the entrepreneurial spirit I was looking for. Eventually, I met one; let's call him Mr Smith. He had a reasonable-sized practice but was essentially a one-man show. We had several meetings and I shared my ideas. He was very keen to join forces and run with my plans. But there was something about him I didn't like. I couldn't put my finger on it exactly, so in the end, I decided against teaming up with him.

Two years later, I met with another accountant who did have the ideal accounting firm, and we joined forces. Part of my plan included writing a book to help drive in new clients. That book became the number one best-selling finance book, and the firm became the fastest growing accounting firm 2 years running. We grew from around $2M to $10M in just 2 years with new offices spread around Australia and over 100 staff.

One day, I was informed by a client that I was being personally criticized in a popular online investor forum. I read the seething and false remarks about me and was intrigued, "Who would write such a thing?" Upon investigation, I discovered the source was—you guessed it—Mr. Smith. I posted a reply on the forum for the record that proved the remarks false and left it at that.

Some time later, as a result of my best-selling book, I was invited to speak at a popular investment expo. While taking a casual walk around the expo stalls to my surprise, there was Mr. Smith with his own exhibition stall, with two staff working with him. I don't particularly care what people think of me, but I always make an effort to clear up any possible misunderstandings so all parties can move forward in harmony or at the very least, with a better understanding of what actually occurred. I decided to take the opportunity to chat with Mr. Smith face-to-face to find out why he had made those comments in that online investor forum.

As it happened, each time I visited his exhibition stand, he was with talking with a client. It wasn't until the end of the expo, when the doors were closed, that I got my opportunity. My personal assistant and I approached him and he greeted my like a long-lost friend; we shook hands as he smiled warmly. We shared some brief small talk about the expo and then I asked him bluntly, "So, what was with those comments you made on that forum?" At first he played dumb, as if he had no idea what I was talking about, and then suddenly the Mr Nice-Guy veneer peeled off and he let loose. I cannot recall his exact words, but it went something like this: "I am going to destroy you and your business. I am going to out-do you and bring you to the ground. There will be nothing left of you in 12 months."

Needless to say, I was shocked. It was such a strange thing to say and so out of the blue. I recall looking at my assistant who was standing there with her mouth open and her chin almost touching the ground.

At that point, I knew exactly what I was dealing with: this guy was a foe. For some reason, that I'll never fathom, he had it in for me. Perhaps it was because I never helped *him* build a national accounting firm, who knows. But one thing I'm certain of, that guy is nuts.

Hitler was also nuts. For some reason, he selected Jews as the ones who needed to be destroyed. And despite having black hair and blue eyes, he thought the optimal human being was one with blonde hair and blue eyes. In his conquest, he killed over six million Jews.

The only difference between the Nutty Accountant and Hitler is the size of their destruction. But they are both foes. Hitler hated Jews and the Nutty Accountant hated a good-looking, modest, black hair, hazel-eyed entrepreneur.

These examples of foes are easy to spot because they attack you directly. You know you need to stay away from them. The more dangerous ones are those who *pretend* to be your "friend" but are really your foe.

Failure to tell the difference can be catastrophic. In fact, every one of my finance and business troubles involved a foe who I thought was a "friend." Let me clarify that last sentence: my financial troubles were the result of Poor Habits; being insolvent and unviable was my doing. However, the degree of insolvency was made far, far worse because of one or more foes.

Later in my business career, when I knew and practiced Rich Habits, I still experienced financial difficulties. Not personally, but in some of my businesses. All these situations were created by foes who I thought were "friends." They lied, cheated, stole and in general caused unnecessary havoc. They were never able to apply the Rich Habits.

And the same is true for others. I've helped many

people and businesses rise from the depths of the Rich Continuum. They all had two things in common: they practiced Poor Habits *and* they had foes in their midst.

Thus, we have another Rich Habits formula:

— RICH HABITS FORMULA —

Poor Habits + Foes = Destitute, misery, heartache, and upset

On a brighter note there is a more uplifting formula:

— RICH HABITS FORMULA —

Rich Habits + Friends = Prosperity, joy, happiness, fun and love

Life Lessons

The lessons I learned during these difficult times are truly priceless. I want to share these lessons with you but I will add a proviso. I'm not sure you will value this information unless you have been stabbed in the back by a foe you thought was a "friend."

It's one of life's lessons that is not truly appreciated until you have gone through the experience. I think in some ways it's like trying to describe colors to a blind person.

So my advice is this: If you are applying the Rich Habits and your situation does NOT improve, you have a foe in your midst working against you.

Identifying Foes

How can you tell a friend from a foe?

Friends help you rise up the Rich Continuum.
Foes try to drag you down.

Based on my personal experiences, here's what you look for:

1. Foes will not practice Rich Habits; they'll keep "accidentally" practicing Poor Habits.

2. Foes stop or hinder any attempt to implement Rich Habits. They may says things like, "But that doesn't fully apply to us" or "Our situation is different."

3. Foes encourage Poor Habits, especially overspending and killer debt. They says things like, "You should buy it, you deserve it," or, "The business really needs this brand-new office; let's sign the lease."

4. You can be yourself around your friends, but with a foe you feel like you have to be on your guard and watch what you say.

5. Friends keep their word most of the time; foes rarely do.

6. Friends complete projects; foes often don't and will blame you or another as the "reason" for an incomplete project.

7. Friends let you be; foes try to control you.

8. Foes offer constructive criticism and excessive praise

that doesn't "feel" right.

9. Foes talk about honesty and integrity yet have none. Friends rarely mention such things because they come naturally.

10. Foes are less successful and able than you but act as if they are better.

11. When in a difficult situation, friends are always there to offer help and support. Foes use it as a means to gain more personal power and push you down.

Foes are like mini-Hitlers. They get their power by taking it from others. Artists, entrepreneurs and creators from all walks of life seek to raise themselves to greater heights through their accomplishments. Mini-Hitlers rise to greater heights by stepping on those they destroy.

The ultimate weapon against a foe is to always be in control of your finances. Never let anyone apply the Rich Habits on your behalf. If you maintain control you can never be brought down.

When you spot the traits of a foe, approach them directly on it. In my experience, the veneer comes off and standing before you is the real person.

If you are unsure whether you have a foe, offer them the "three strikes." It works this way: You state very clearly, without any emotion, the key points you are concerned with, such as failed projects, concern over certain conduct, such as constantly violating the Rich Habits—whatever it might be. Then you offer them the ultimatum: Three more strikes and you're out.

A person is either a friend or a foe, never in between. Sure, people can have a bad day and life has its ups and downs. But a friend pulls in the same direction most of the time. A Foe rarely pulls in the same direction. You might think a person can be neutral, neither pulling or pushing, but why have someone on your team who doesn't contribute to the overall goal? You're better off with nobody than a neutral person, as that person is closer to being a foe than a friend.

It may be hard to fathom, if you have sailed through life and business without being a victim of a mini-Hitler. I honestly hope that it continues that way and you consider this chapter nothing more than a writer's personal rant.

But if, on the other-hand, your goals and plans are taking too long or failing, review the traits above and quietly analyze your "friends"—it might be the answer that will clear the highway to your own prosperity and allow you to soar up the Rich Continuum, unhindered.

These vital Rich Habits summarize this important chapter:

— RICH HABIT —

The Rich are impossible to deceive because they maintain financial control.

The Rich identify and eliminate foe influence.

— POOR HABITS —

The Poor can be easily deceived because they lack any financial control.

The Poor cannot tell the difference between friend or foe and thus suffer.

15

INVESTING

I expect, by now, you're itching to start allocating towards your Investment Fund, if you haven't already. Once that fund starts accumulating, there will come a time when you need to put the money to work.

Uncertainty of what to invest in and the fear of losing money are the most common barriers people run into when it comes to investing. The purpose of this chapter is to provide you with fundamental knowledge of the subject of "investing." That way, you can confidently decide what type of investing style you wish to pursue for financial success.

The first and most important fundamental on the subject of investing is to know what investing is!

The word "invest" comes from the Latin word *investire*, which means *to clothe*. Our Rich Habits definition is simply:

— RICH HABITS DEFINITION —

Invest is using money to buy something that provides a profit or income or both.

With an understanding of this, we can separate the different types of activities an investor can pursue or avoid.

Gambler

Investing is very different to gambling, which is defined as *betting on an uncertain outcome in the hope of winning.* As an investor, you should know the potential outcomes and your investments should make a profit. Knowing the outcome means you fully understand the risks involved and are prepared to take that risk. This requires an investor to have a plan and follow it; there is no *hope* involved with investing. An investor who is uncertain about the possible outcomes, who doesn't have a plan and who *hopes* to make a profit, is a gambler not an investor.

Trader

The word "trade" means *the act or process of buying and selling; the exchange of goods.* A trader is one who makes money through the *act* of buying and *selling.* An investor makes money through buying and keeping and doesn't necessarily need to sell. If you look closely again at the definition of "invest," it does not mention the word "selling."

A trader *must* sell to make a profit. This means the trader either buys something that is undervalued and then sells it when it goes up, or the trader buys something and improves its value and then sells it.

There are many things a person can trade. You can buy

a run-down property and increase its value by renovating it and then sell it for a profit. An experienced share trader looks for undervalued companies, buys their shares and sells them when they go up. I once knew a guy who used to buy run-down cars. He'd fix them up, give them a new coat of paint or a new motor and sell them for a profit. He would often make $2,000 per car. Today, with the accessibility of the internet and sites like eBay and Craigslist, people can trade all sorts of things very easily. There is no shortage of opportunity for things to trade and ways to trade them.

Dealmaker

A "deal" is *an agreement or transaction that benefits all the parties involved*. A dealmaker is one who *creates* deals by joining two or more people together and profiting from the deal personally.

A dealmaker differs from a trader and investor in that they don't need to use money to make money. Instead, they seek opportunities and match people to opportunities. The key attribute of a dealmaker is the skill of negotiating.

Here's an example of dealmaking using property. Let's say a dealmaker found some land that was perfect for developing several brand-new apartments. The dealmaker contacts the landowner and gets the owner's agreement to sell him the land. He secures it for a fair price with a small deposit and a formal contract. Using his connections, the dealmaker convinces several investors to participate in the development by each investing cash. The dealmaker then organizes finance for the whole project through a bank.

With finance in place, he hires a project manager who oversees the development. Once complete and sold, the dealmaker receives a percentage of the profits, as do the initial investors. Everybody wins!

Investor

An "investor" is *someone who uses money to buy something that produces a profit or income or both.* The whole essence of investing is to accumulate. This is the most passive method of investing and is often called "buy and hold." As an investor, you let *time* do the work. Your investments increase in value over time, which improves your solvency.

Learning additional skills such as negotiation and how to buy below current market value can improve the result of your investments. If you further your education in your chosen field, you can possibly pick the market highs and lows. Selling near the market peaks and buying again at market lows improves your result and increases your solvency, but given enough time, it is not necessary to get the result of increased value—time does it for you.

By explaining the different roles above, there may be one or more that appeal to you and your personality. Decide which is the best one for you, taking into consideration how much time you have to dedicate to the role.

Types of Roles

To get your money working for you, and to beat inflation, requires that you take action. Even an investor who accumulates investments must still take action to put their money to work. There is, however, a difference in how the profit is made.

An investor uses *time* as his primary tool for profit. The longer the investment is owned, the more it is worth. A trader uses *skills* in buying or improving an investment as well as the skill of selling—these require more action than an investor. A dealmaker uses his contacts and foresight to make money; there is usually less action involved than that of the trader but more than that of an investor. A gambler of course uses neither skill nor time nor foresight—he just hopes.

	Investor	Trader	Dealmaker
Skills	Discipline & Patience	Market Knowledge	Negotiation
Activity	Passive	Active	Active
Key Concept	Accumulate	Exchange	Opportunity
Timeframe	Long-term (10 + years)	Short-term (< year)	Length of deal
Needs	Money	Money & Time	Mostly Time
Investment Vehicles	• Property • Shares • Business • Property Developments	• Property Renovations • Undervalued Shares • Share Trading • Property Developments • Anything that can be purchased cheaply, improved and sold for a profit	• Property Deals • Business Acquisitions • Business Deals • Property Developments

It doesn't matter which of the above roles you choose; you should at the very least be an *investor*. If you desire to trade or make deals, that only adds to the rewards you receive as an investor.

Allocation of Profits

When selling investments, the profits should be allocated, like all income, with the majority of it going back into investments. Income derived from investments is allocated as usual. For example; rent received from property is income and increases viability; however, if the property is sold a bulk of the profit is best allocated to investments.

Now let's cover the main investing vehicles.

Property

Property goes up in value when there is a demand for that type of property. If people want to live in a particular area and the property supply is low, there will be demand and that will drive prices up.

Supply and demand can fluctuate causing prices to fall, but when the following selection criteria of property is followed, you will eventually see a return of demand and steadily rising prices.

The simple Rich Habits criteria for investment property include the following: proximity to schools, public transport, parks, and recreational facilities and located in a place where people work and want to live. These areas, despite any economic downturn, will usually rebound over time because of these basic qualities, and demand will return.

Share Market

The share market as a whole follows an economic cycle much like the property market. The major difference, however, is its higher level of volatility.

There are basically two different ways to research the share market to help you decide which company is best to invest your money in: fundamental analysis and technical analysis.

Fundamental Analysis: This research focuses on the company's performance in the marketplace, its financial statements and overall profits. The purpose of fundamental analysis is to look for undervalued stocks that are likely to grow in value in the future. These days, ample information is available online for free. There are also many courses that teach basic and advanced levels of fundamental analysis.

Technical Analysis: This type of research focuses purely on the share price. It is based on the premise that the share price will follow certain chart patterns that have a predictable outcome. If you enjoy numbers and graphs, this method might appeal to you; it is for the most part a method used by traders rather than investors and is usually more short-term.

There are many courses available that teach both basic and advanced techniques, and there are numerous companies that provide the software and information online.

Business

Whether you are starting a business or investing in a going concern with the intention of improving it, you need to understand some business basics.

If investing in a business being run or started by another person, the first step is finding out if that *person* has successfully built a business before or successfully done something similar. From my experience, people often invest in a wonderful product or service and don't consider the person or people involved, as much. Yet the success of any business rests on the shoulders of those who run it. No matter how wonderful the idea, it can fail when put under the guidance of an incompetent person.

The second point of research for any business, whether established or not, is to find out what people want. This is the key to every business I have ever built or consulted. Does the business or product solve a problem? And if so, what are people willing to pay to have that problem solved? Are there enough people who want that problem solved? If you know these answers and it's worthwhile, then the business is likely to be a winner. As for established businesses, just ask the current clients what they want and you'll get valuable insight into what to provide them.

If you want to know more about building and running a successful a business, check out Boom University at tonymelvin.com.

Strategy

The key to successful investing is having and following a strategy. The word "strategy" means *a carefully devised plan of action to achieve a goal*. It comes from the Greek word *strategos*, which means *to lead an army*.

Any investor, trader or dealmaker should have a strategy. The way to make a million dollars is to have a strategy that will get you there: a step-by-step plan of action that takes you closer to your goal with every step you take.

Investing should be looked upon as a game. The type of game you play is the strategy you implement. Your role in the game is as an investor, trader or dealmaker. Using this analogy, you can see that if a person suddenly changes roles in a game, they can get into trouble, like the goalkeeper in a soccer game who suddenly decides to be the centre forward. This would not only annoy the other players, it may just lose them the game. A similar problem occurs if you suddenly change games. Imagine a soccer player who switches to playing basketball half-way through a game; he would be thrown off the playing field.

Therefore, with your strategy in place, don't go changing halfway through, and don't change roles. If you are an investor, stick to investing and the strategy you've worked out. Don't suddenly start trading your investments for a quick buck.

This doesn't mean you can't be a dealmaker or trader if you are an investor. What it means is that you need to have an effective strategy for each of the investing styles, and don't mix them up. If you are accumulating assets, don't use those assets to trade. Keep the activities separate and stick to your strategy.

It's a common pitfall. Failure as an investor can often be traced back to not being an investor at all but starting off as an investor and then switching to a trader or dealmaker without mastering the skills necessary.

For example, a property is purchased as a buy-and-hold investment. The initial plan is to keep it and let it grow. Then you hear of a neighbor who developed a property similar to yours and made a fortune. Without any education of how to do it, you decide to do the same. Your property has increased in value and you borrow money to start developing. During the development stage, the property market takes a fall. You're forced to sell the whole development to avoid going under. The experience has left you insolvent. Now you consider "investing" to be risky. This is not true. Changing the game or your role in it is risky.

The other important lesson from the example above is that *before* you play a game, you should understand the rules of that game. Before you implement an investment strategy, you need to know the rules of that strategy and how it works. There are many successful investors who teach courses that cover all types of investment strategies. It's important, however, that you can tell the difference between the genuine teachers and the frauds.

Money Talks

In today's society, someone is considered successful if they drive a nice car and live in a nice house. But as you know, such items can be bought on credit, giving the appearance of wealth when there is none.

Money talks, but the question is: *whose money is it?* A person can be insolvent and yet *appear* to have money.

Therefore, it's important to be able to tell the difference between genuine educators and charlatans; it's also important to know if the advice offered is based on facts or opinion.

Separating Opinion from Fact

We get a constant barrage of information from the media regarding the economy, the rise and fall of the share market and property values. Most of it is sensationalized and filled with dire warnings and impending doom. Rarely is the news today encouraging; this applies not just to financial news but to all news. The fact that it is even called news is a misnomer; it should be called "threats and gossip."

These are bold statements but they can be justified by the fact that much of what we hear is opinion and not fact.

- Fact = something that actually exists or has occurred

- Opinion = a conclusion or judgment

The word "fact" originates from the Latin word *facere* which means *to do*. The word "opinion" derives from the Latin word *opinari* meaning *to think*.

Firstly, you need to deal with facts and then make your own opinions. Making decisions based on the opinions of another is using their judgments in place of your own.

When it comes to managing finances and making investment decisions, the biggest hurdle most people need to overcome is believing other people's opinions, when taken on board as fact, these opinions stop them from taking action.

Lack of time or money are often used as an excuse as to why an investor doesn't succeed. This is not true! The main reason people don't succeed is due to lack of belief in themselves and their strategy. The self-confidence a person has is often sucked out of them by others and the media.

It's vital that you are able to identify the difference between fact and opinion so that you can maintain your confidence and certainty. Nothing can stop you if you believe in yourself 100%.

Facts can be seen—they have happened! For the investor, this means statistics, financial records, solvency, viability, etc. These things can be proven. If a company made one million dollars, show me the bank statement. If the money is there, it's a fact. If a real estate agent tells me that prices have risen 10% and will continue to do so, firstly, prove to me that they have risen 10% (facts) and secondly, show me the data (facts) used to form the *opinion* that they will continue to grow. Using this data, I will form my own opinion.

Developing the skill of separating fact from opinion can save you a fortune, and make you one. When people come to a conclusion or make a judgment about a situation, it has to be based on *facts*. In order to make your own judgment, you need to knows those facts.

Here's an example: Someone tells you that John Doe, who lives down the street, is a crook and a thief. The smart thing to do at this point is to ask, "*What did he do that made him a crook?*" If evidence can be shown that he did such and such, then that is fact; if it is a story the person heard from another, then it could just be an opinion. Further research is needed to *prove* the story, which at this point is just gossip.

As an investor, someone might tell you that property prices are going to dive so you shouldn't invest. This is an opinion; finding out why they have come to such a conclusion is the only way for you to decide whether to agree with such an opinion.

An investor needs to be wary of those who have a vested interest in selling or advising. An advisor will recommend investments based on the training they have had or the amount of commission they will earn. As cynical as this sounds, you cannot discount the fact that when someone makes their living from commissions based on advice they offer, that advice might be biased.

This doesn't mean that everyone who is trying to sell property, shares or managed funds is lying or not telling the truth or is twisting facts. What it means is that you need to be aware of this and make your judgment based on the facts, not on what you are told.

Investorphobia

Investorphobia is a word I've coined to describe the fear manifested by certain people who cannot, under any circumstances, see the potential of an investment opportunity. All they see are the risks. Economic turmoil creates more investorphobia. The media thrive on it and seem to do nothing but feed it. The sufferers of investorphobia spread their fears to others continuously. Yet their fears are based on opinions and rarely contain any judgment of their own. Sufferers will list all the reasons NOT to invest and all the horror stories to go with them without been asked for such "advice." Sufferers of this disease have either had a bad investing experience themselves and remind everybody about it, or they have had no experience at all, yet they suffer and are themselves most likely sitting in the middle of the Rich Continuum, at Broke, or worse, they are insolvent and sinking towards Poor.

You can probably think of examples of people like this. The best thing to do is ignore them. The information they so readily share is tarnished with their own fears and is not worth listening to. Experience has proven to me that it's also quite fruitless to try to change their mind. Tell them to read a good book on the subject, but don't waste your time trying to convince them. Just get on with investing yourself. Such people, even when you provide proof of your success with a Solvency Graph that goes up the wall, will say, "You're lucky because when old Joe invested in the stock market, oh boy, you know what happen? Well, he lost ….” They just won’t get it.

As a final word on this important point of fact versus opinion, as a master of your own financial destiny, you’ll find it much easier dealing with positive people who think like you. Anyone or anything that discourages you makes the journey that little bit harder. Therefore, my advice is to stay away from bad news. I sold my TV when I was 19 years old, and I still do not own one to this day. I have an awesome cinema set up in my home because I enjoy a good movie, but I don’t watch TV. Some wonder how I keep up with world news and events; that is very easy today with the internet, but the important thing is I decide what information I want, rather than being bombarded with bad news every day.

You know that your goals are increasing solvency and viability—so don’t let anybody sway you from that course. Stick to your goals and your chosen investing game. Beware of vested interests, always check people’s opinions against actual facts and make your own judgment.

— RICH HABIT —

The Rich separate fact from opinion and use their own judgement.

— POOR HABIT —

The Poor confuse facts and opinions and make mistakes, or fail to act.

Economic Cycles

In recent times, due to falling property prices in some parts of the world, many people have found themselves in a situation where their mortgage is more than the value of their property. Does this mean the person should sell their property? Does it mean they now have a "killer debt" that needs to be paid off?

The answer to both questions is: "No!"

Dropping Property Values Affecting Solvency

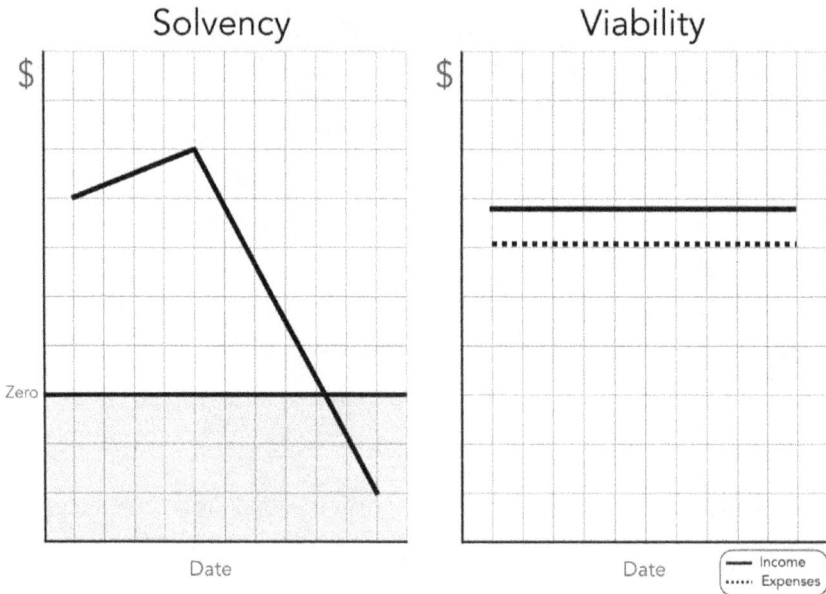

If your property has dropped in value, selling it should be your last resort. Just because your solvency has fallen doesn't mean you need to start selling everything—even if you are insolvent. What happens to your solvency if you sell the asset? Nothing! You'll still be in the same situation. Some might argue that at least you wouldn't lose any more money if the property continues to fall in value; yes that's true, but by selling it, you wouldn't benefit from the increase if it goes up in value either.

You only lose money when you sell something for a loss. If you hold on to an asset that is needed (like a property), you have a good chance of recouping your "loss" and increasing your solvency.

Property markets, share markets and economies in general all work on a cyclic basis. They go up and they go down. The most important thing is to maintain your viability. If you are viable, you can last until the next upward cycle when prices recover.

As an example, take a look at the following graph of the S&P 500 (short for Standard & Poor's 500). Standard & Poor is a company that publishes financial information and the S&P 500 is an average of the share prices of the 500 major companies based in the U.S. It can be seen that while the prices generally go up, they move in waves.

S&P 500 Index
From 1950 to 2016

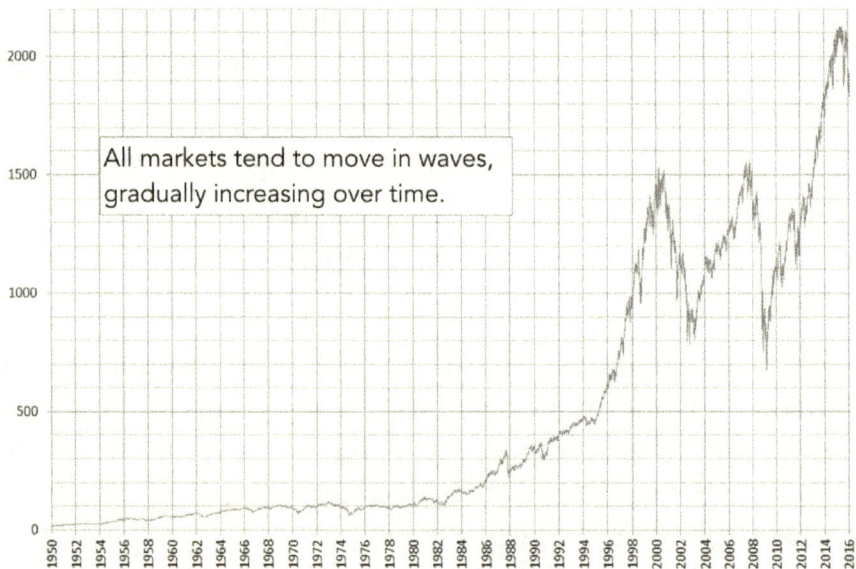

All markets tend to move in waves, gradually increasing over time.

All economies work in cycles. As an investor who is accumulating assets, the principle one must understand is that *time in the market* is more important than trying to *time the market*.

Remember, you don't suddenly change your game: an investor *accumulates*. Therefore any drop in market values should be looked upon as an opportunity to acquire *more* investments at a discount! Adding more properties (that fit the Rich Habits criteria) to your property portfolio is the way to go.

16

RICH HABITS APPLIED TO NATIONS AND POLITICS

The Rich Habits apply to individuals and businesses. They also apply more broadly to a community, county, state, and even an entire country.

They should all be *solvent*, meaning they have more assets than debt. They should be *viable*, that is, the money received from taxes should be more than the money spent by the government. The treasury department should *allocate* money to healthcare, infrastructure, education, the arts, and technology, to name a few, with the purpose of enhancing the future of that society.

However, the above rarely happens. Politicians make promises to make things better, yet they are hindered by the Poor Habits of their predecessors. No matter what laws are passed, if those in power fail to replace Poor Habits with Rich Habits on a national scale, we will continue to witness economic turmoil.

A "deficit" means *expenses are more than the money available*. It is really another word for unviable. At the time of writing, here are the basic statistics of the major and newsworthy economies:

Poor Habits of a Nation
Nation values in USD Billion

Country	Government Debt	Government Income from Taxes	Government Spending	Unviability (Deficit)
USA	2,060	3,350	4,011	-661
Per Citizen	$6,311	$10,262	$12,287	-$2,025
China	4,650	1,800	2,147	-347
Per Citizen	$3,333	$1,290	$1,539	-$249
U.K	2,060	962	1,031	-69
Per Citizen	$31,111	$14,528	$15,571	-$1,042
Japan	11,700	1,480	1,810	-330
Per Citizen	$92,457	$11,695	$14,303	-$2,608
Australia	629	333	357	-24
Per Citizen	$25,523	$13,512	$14,486	-$974
Greece	337	79	133	-54
Per Citizen	$31,128	$7,297	$12,285	-$4,988

Data Sources: usdebtclock.org, stats.oecd.org, wikipedia.org, countryeconomy.com, tradingeconomics.com and Government Website of each country.

All these countries are unviable. If you want to see where your country is right now, in real time, take a look at tonylink.me/world-debt, and for a detailed view of the USA, visit tonylink.me/usa-debt. It's a sobering look at the economy.

As we have covered, if you overspend, it must be taken from the future "you." If a country overspends, the money borrowed today is really taken from the future generation. Unless a country is viable, how can they ever repay their debt? How can it ever be solvent?

These national Poor Habits must change. The process for a country is the same as that for the individual; 1) recognize Rich Habits exist, 2) start to allocate and aim for viability, 3) aim for improving solvency. It might seem like an impossible task, but it isn't. Hong Kong managed to do just that—in 2001, their national debt was $5.5 billion; now it's $193 million—that's over 96% reduction in debt in 16 years.

You've perhaps heard of "austerity measures." The word "austerity" comes from a word that means *severe* and in the economic sense it means *difficult economic conditions created by government, to reduce a budget deficit (unviability), especially by reducing public expenditure.* In other words, they tighten spending in an effort to get viable. This is a step in the right direction, but due to a lack of understanding about money, and a lack of trust or faith of those in power (who, after all, have been practicing Poor Habits), austerity measures can lead to protests, as it did in Greece in May 2011. Over 100,000 people stood on the steps of parliament in Athens to oppose the tightened spending. The problem, of course, started much earlier, and the degree of severity of tighter spending is in direct proportion how far down the Rich Continuum a country has fallen. At the time, Greece could not pay its debts, so they negotiated with the International Money Fund (IMF) and other creditors. They actually followed the *Solvency System* by getting a 50% reduction in debts and a reduced interest rate but their biggest mistake was they also borrowed an additional €110 billion from the IMF, which they had already done the year prior. So their solution to being unviable and insolvent was to borrow more money and become more insolvent. That is a Poor Habit, and

Greece really has made it a habit because they repeated the action in 2012, 2014, 2015, 2017. They keep borrowing money to "solve" their unviability. In contrast to Hong Kong, in 2001, Greece had a national debt of $146 billion, which has more than doubled to $337 billion today. Greece is not the only country to do this, of course, but it's a most recent newsworthy example.

If the entire nation understood Rich Habits, even the basic concept of the Rich Triangle and the Poor Triangle, and if each and every person was asked to vote on how the money should be allocated, and given a say in the matter, I believe there would be less protests, as I'm sure the citizens of Greece want a viable and solvent country. To make a change of this magnitude requires that *everyone* understands the process. Education and understanding are the solution to any problem; force and ignorance only make it worse.

You might wonder what can *you* really do about it? Well, you have more influence than you realize. Explaining the concepts of solvency, viability, and allocation to someone who is in a state of confusion about their own finances provides clarity and relief; helping a business owner work out how to be viable does wonders for their self-esteem and confidence. And so it goes, on up to your local government official, the mayor, your congressman, senator, prime minister, president, king or queen.

Most important of all, each of us can educate our youth, for those are the leaders of tomorrow, and there is no better way to fight the Poor Plague, than to make the next generation immune before they venture out into this crazy economic world. I bet you wish you knew this information a lot earlier than now? Well, let's make sure they learn it, and let's help them turn the tide. The best way to do that is to set an example yourself, by rising up the Rich Continuum. If you lead the way, others will naturally follow. In the end, it all starts with you.

— RICH HABIT —

The Rich teach Rich Habits by example and encourage others to do the same.

— POOR HABIT —

The Poor teach Poor Habits by example and think the Rich are lucky.

17

MY STORY

I have spoken in front of thousands of people around Australia, Asia and the USA, teaching the principles of business management, investing and the Rich Habits, and when I do, I am often asked two questions, "How did you make the money to pay off your debts?" and "Where did you start?"

This chapter will feed your curiosity if you happen to have the same questions.

Financial disaster hit me around late 2001. It took just under two years to pay back the bulk of my creditors. The remaining few were paid off on payment terms. I still had some personal debt at that time, so I wasn't quite solvent, but I'd swam a long way and was near the surface.

How I actually got into such financial trouble is not worthy of detail except to say that I had no awareness of the Rich Habits and constantly practiced Poor Habits. I was making more money than ever just prior to my demise. My biggest mistake was believing that it didn't matter how much money I spent, I could always make more money. And spend I did!

Reality came crashing down one day after the failed sale of my business when I woke up realizing I had sold everything and was still in debt. The business sale was supposed to be my ticket to solvency. In fact, I was set to pocket a tidy sum that would not only pay off all my debt, but leave me with a nice surplus. However, my Poor Habits created bad business habits and I'd "counted my chickens before they'd hatched." Assuming the sale was imminent, I wound up the business activities and waited for the transaction to take place. It was a total shock when that last easy ticket didn't materialize. Not only did the buyer pull out, the business had become worthless because I'd suspended activities during the delays in the selling process. A simple viability graph on the wall at that very moment would have told me to *keep making money!*

So, there I was, resting on the floor of a bedroom at a friend's place, my temporary residence, wondering how on earth I was going to get out of this situation!

I knew I was insolvent. I also knew I was going backwards every month. I'd promised my creditors payment when the business sold. I realized I'd have to tell them the bad news soon but I didn't want to break it to them without also providing them with some good news: a solution.

I simply had to make lots of money, and to do it, I would have to work hard. I blamed nobody. I realized that if I could get myself into debt, then I could get out of it. Doing the exact opposite of what I was doing would be a good start, which meant tight money control.

My first goal was to get viable, which meant I needed about $4000 (after tax). So, I set out to make at least that every month. This included making enough to cover my living expenses and the interest on my debt.

The first thing I did was secure regular income. I chose evening work, which enabled me to work on another income source during the day. I visited Len and Steve, friends of mine who had a property business. I knew they had a telemarketing team working evenings, cold-calling clients. They had a couple of ladies who would come in for 3 hours and make some calls. These ladies had been doing it for a few years and would always make some appointments, but in my opinion, the result could be monitored and improved. So, I made an offer to my friends. Pay me $300 a week and I'll improve the telemarketing results. I would work from 4 p.m. until 9 p.m. Monday to Friday and monitor the telemarketing and improve results. I had already calculated that if they paid me $300 a week for 50 weeks, it equated to $15,000 per year. They would only need to sell one property to make up for the cost. If I didn't improve the results in three months, I'd leave. I put this all in writing to them and sat patiently while they read it. After reading it, they wanted to talk privately and asked me to step out of the room for a minute.

I should mention at this point that you do need to sell yourself. Nobody is going to give you the perfect job. You need to decide what you want, what hours you are willing to work and what you're prepared to *give* in return. As part of my offer, I explained my skills. I never assumed they knew all my strengths—so there's another tip: Don't be afraid to brag.

After a few minutes, I was invited back into the room. They sat me down and said they liked the idea. Steve had one question, however. "The $300 a week, is that enough?"

The truth is, it wasn't enough, not by a long shot, but I'd worked out what I thought was reasonable and what covered the living expenses of food, rent and gas. I knew I was going to be working during the day to make more money so getting $300 each week meant I could survive.

Steve said, "Tony, we'll do it on one condition: we'll pay you $500 a week." Like I said, these guys were my friends; they still are.

This was quite a humiliating experience for me at the time, as several months prior to this, I was doing deals with these guys and here I was asking for a few hundred bucks just to survive. I mention this because you may feel the same way at some point. My advice is: get over it! Swallow your pride and get on with the job of getting solvent. Feeling sorry for yourself or expecting any sympathy is a waste of time. If you're in debt, you have to get out of it— and this journey, if you follow my advice, will change your life forever. Taking responsibility for one's mistakes and making good your promise despite all odds is what builds character. You'll get more respect from people by lifting your head up and pushing your shoulders back than you will by feeling sorry for yourself. Please don't take this as an accusation; it's the kindest advice I could give—don't ever think you're a failure or a victim. Besides, *I know* you're not because you're reading this book!

With my new-found role as Telemarketing Manager, I set out to make more money during the day. I'd recently met a guy named Bill, who had a commercial cleaning business that specialized in cleaning kitchens and ventilation systems. Bill needed some help on a job, so I joined him, along with a friend of mine named Scott. I made $200 for 4 hours of work. It was very dirty work, I might add, but there was hardly any material costs. Bill had quoted about $2000 for this job. Immediately, I could see a business opportunity.

As it turned out, Bill was happy to remain a one-man band, but Scott and I could see the potential for a big business. So, we started a commercial cleaning business!

The first thing I did was design a simple promotional piece, which took about 3 minutes. I printed off a couple hundred flyers on orange paper because it was the only paper I had (one of the few remaining "assets" from my previous business!). We hand wrote the mailing addresses on envelopes and sent them to restaurants around Sydney. We used some of the money we made from our first job with Bill to pay for postage.

From that first mailing, we got several calls and did about 4 quotes. One of the quotes came through and we made $500 for two hours work. Scott and I took $100 each and put the rest towards more promotion. Because this was our own business, we planned the jobs to suit my work schedule. Also, because it was the restaurant industry, the best time to clean was in the morning when the restaurants were closed, which fit perfectly with my telemarketing position in the evenings.

This little business started to take off. Within a few weeks, we hired Scott's mother to handwrite the envelopes and send them to restaurants for us. After about 6 weeks, we bought a beat-up van to travel in (so we didn't get our own cars dirty). We kept up the promotion and did the jobs ourselves. I remember around this time, my working schedule was insane. I would do a job at 3 a.m. in the morning; finish around 7 a.m.; eat breakfast; start another cleaning job at 8 a.m.; finish at 1 p.m.; sleep for 2 hours; put on my business suit and rock up as the Telemarketing Manager at 4 p.m.; work until 9 p.m.; go home and sleep for 3 hours and do it all again!

There were days when I wouldn't sleep at all, and I would stay awake for 40 hours straight. Often, I would take a catnap in my car. Sometimes, I would turn up at the telemarketing job, black from head to toe in my dirty clothes, take a shower in the office restroom and then put on my suit. I was a bit like Michael J. Fox in that eighties movie, *The Secret of My Success*, always changing clothes from one role to the next! But I did whatever it took to get the jobs done. This mad schedule, however, was only required for about 3 months. The business continued to expand, so we started hiring staff. In its first year, this little cleaning business turned over more than $600,000, and by that time we had 4 vehicles and 6 staff. We expanded into ventilation installations and emergency ventilation repairs. All from sending out that same simple flyer (which by the way was always printed on orange paper because that's what worked! It wasn't changed at all for the first 3 years). After the initial 3 months, my role became managing the finances of the business, doing quotes and collecting money. Scott ran the cleaning teams and made sure the jobs got done. This meant that I could focus more on building another income stream.

With the cleaning business doing well, I looked for more opportunity in the property business I was working for with Len and Steve. I had expanded and improved the telemarketing team as promised. A little investigation revealed that it was possible for me to do the same with the sales team as I had done with the telemarketing team. They had no Sales Manager at that time and I knew I could improve the results. Once again, I approached Steve and Len, this time with an offer to pay me commission only on property sales and I'd improve the results. I was still getting a $500 retainer but I said, "That could be part of the commission; we'll consider it an advance." For them, it was a risk-free proposition, much like the first offer. I made sure, however, that I replaced myself with a new Telemarketing Manager before leaving that role. The new person was paid the same as I was, only now the role was proven to be worthwhile and cost-effective, so that was easy.

After two months, property sales had doubled and things were going great. The only difficulty was I had to wait until the properties were built before I received my commission. While some were three months away, others were as much as twelve months away. Although the money would come eventually, I needed it now! Len and Steve, being the great guys they are, came to my aid and advanced some of my commissions which enabled me to handle a large portion of my debt.

So, there you have it: that was the first eight months or so of how I tackled my debts. I share this with you to highlight one thing—*it takes hard work.* Looking back now, I could have done it a different way and possibly could have done it quicker. But I was doing the best I could with the resources I had at the time. Today, I think I could pay off $300,000 even faster, but that's only because I have the experience. Therefore, I wouldn't compare yourself to me; you probably have better ways to make money that don't require such an insane schedule—but whatever you do, don't idle. Work hard and use every possible moment to improve your situation and get solvent.

The more *in*solvent you are, the more you have to work at it. I was in a real dire situation and had to really work hard to keep the creditors at bay, especially the ones who had taken legal action against me.

Looking back at it all now, I can honestly say that those times were fun. Yes, we worked hard and Scott and I did some wild jobs back in those days. Despite the hard work and long hours, when I think of those times, it makes me smile. It also makes me appreciate what I have now: the luxury of being a writer and spending time with my family.

I hope that by sharing this with you, it helps in some way. I personally set out to generate four separate income streams that would each handle my debts in twelve months. I ended up with three that worked. If you're in deep water, at the bottom of the Rich Continuum, I suggest you do the same.

— RICH HABIT —

The Rich are proactive.

The Rich are willing to work hard.

— POOR HABIT —

The Poor blame.

The Poor avoid hard work.

18

THE RICH REBELLION

$\triangle$

You are now armed with full awareness that Rich Habits exist, what they are and how to soar up the Rich Continuum. As you apply what you have learned, and your solvency improves, and you eliminate your killer debt, you will notice others who also need the same help. With that in mind, I have a proposition for you. First, let me ask you a few questions.

How would you like to be a part of something that could change the financial destiny of millions?

How would you like to flourish and prosper by helping others do the same?

How would you like to rid the world of the unnecessary burden of killer debt and the stress associated with money?

Money causes stress, quarrels, marital problems, fights and even wars. But it doesn't have to. If people understood and developed Rich Habits, such things could be avoided.

The world today is imbued with Poor Habits. Spend now, pay later is the motto many live buy. And by "many," I mean all strata of life: the individual, small businesses, large corporations and governments.

What can turn this tide? How can society change from practicing Poor Habits to embracing the Rich Habits? Who is going to do it?

I am.

And I'd like you to join me, because I'm going to need a lot of help.

To make such an impact on the world, to reach everyone from school kids to retirees, requires a movement. Not just another book, and definitely not another gimmick like *"The Secrets of the Wealthy."* No, this is going to require much more than a superficial, feel-good message.

It's going to take rebellion.

This book is the first weapon in the arsenal of tools I intend to create. The Rich Habits board game will provide an instant cure to the Poor Habits Plague. And more books and online courses will come. I want to unleash these upon the world, change the tide and make a difference.

Any great battle, for a chance of success, needs two things: 1) a clear strategy and 2) troops.

Strategy: My strategy is very simple: Let's make everyone aware of the Rich Habits, for that alone starts their journey up the Rich Continuum. This is easily achieved by this book alone, and with the Rich Habits board game, we'll be well on our way.

Troops: Although this is a rebellion, unlike other

uprisings, where troops are asked to kill or maim, our rebellion requires no violence—it's a Rich Rebellion and has the pure intention of *helping everyone rise up the Rich Continuum, free from financial stress and worry.* Now, if you participate in a rebellion, that makes you a rebel, does it not? In this case, a Rich Rebel. I like the sound of that! Below outlines how you can join in this Rich Rebellion.

Rebel Affiliate

Tell others about this book and how it has helped you. But don't give them your copy; instead, send them to the website and *make them buy their own.* Alternatively, you can buy several copies in bulk and give them away as gifts, if you wish. If you'd like to earn an extra buck (and improve your viability), then become an affiliate and earn commissions on everything your referrals purchase. Find out more at myrichhabits.com/rebellion.

Rich Habits Distributor

As an official distributor, you are able to purchase all Rich Habits products at wholesale rates and sell these in your local area. Training includes how to organize, promote and present live events, as well as how to conduct game nights. As more products and services are released, you'll expand your income streams, while helping others discover the Rich Habits. The time spent in this role is flexible; you can do it as a part-time hobby to earn a few extra bucks or as a full-time career. For more information, visit myrichhabits.com/rebellion.

Certified Rich Habits Coach

Imagine spending your day helping others rise up the Rich Continuum. It is truly a rewarding "job" because you get to rejoice in their wins, as if they were your own. And you get paid to do it!

Full training is provided and you become certified to help both individuals and businesses learn and implement the Rich Habits. You are also trained and certified as a Rich Habits Distributor so you can easily build your client base and make additional income from selling products.

For more information, visit myrichhabits.com/rebellion.

Rich Habits Alliance Network

We intend to build a network of like-minded professionals that will help Rich Rebels on their journey up the Rich Continuum. A Rich Habits Alliance Member is a certified business or individual who has been trained on the Rich Habits principles. Members of the Rich Habits Community will be encouraged to seek help from Alliance Members when in need of professional advice and assistance. Exclusive territories are available around the world in the following industries:

- Bookkeeping

- Accounting

- Finance Broker

- Quantity Surveyors

- Lawyers

- Stockbrokers

- Property Investment

- Investment Education & Services

- Business Consulting

- Business Services

For more information, visit myrichhabits.com/rebellion.

Call to Arms

A "call to arms" is defined as *to prepare for confrontation*. And the definition of a "rebel" is *a person who resists authority, control, or convention*. It comes from a Latin word meaning *war*.

As a team, we are declaring war against Poor Habits and killer debt. We're going to bring them under control and eliminate them.

It's going to be a fun ride.

It will, no doubt, leave a legacy.

I wonder how many people we can reach?

I wonder how fast we can reach them?

I know for certain I'll do it faster with a bunch of likeminded rebels.

Are you a rebel? If so, come join me.

19
RICH HABITS COMMUNITY & COACHING

Reading this book is your first step on your journey towards the top of the Rich Continuum. Often, the journey can be lonely, and if you are slowly crawling your way up from Poor towards Broke, it can be tough staying motivated. With that in mind, I've created several different support services to help you on your way. These range from free services—where you can get all the information and help you need to do it your own—to personal coaching, where you can get more direct help.

For full details and pricing, visit myrichhabits.com.

Rich Habits Free Community

As the name suggests, this Rich Habits Community is free. Members can download the *Rich Habits Guidebook* and the *Rich Habits Toolkit*, with spreadsheets, example letters, and other goodies promised in this book.

You can also share your wins from applying the Rich Habits and encourage other members to do the same. If you need help, you can reach out to the community.

Rich Habits Coaching Community

This exclusive coaching community is a place where you'll get help, encouragement and support, with questions answered by Tony every week so you can apply the Rich Habits and eliminate killer debt fast.

If you can relate to any of these below, you will benefit from this coaching community:

1. You're stressed out about debt.

2. You feel like you're constantly struggling, no matter how much money you are making.

3. You're worried about money.

4. No matter how hard you work, you can't seem to get ahead.

5. You feel guilt or regret about spending money.

6. You've been ripped off by "friends" or business partners.

You get access to training videos, downloads and support from Tony and the entire Rich Habits Coaching Community.

With the Rich Habits Coaching Community, you'll discover everything you need to eliminate killer debt and create Rich Habits. You can easily review each video lesson as many times as you need. This education will provide you with the foundation that will make you a true

Rebel, well on your way to solvency.

Rich Habits Personal Coaching

For those of you who want a more personalized approach, you can opt for the Personal Coaching program. Your Rich Habits Coach will take you through the *Rich Habits Guidebook* and address each step. This is ideal for those who feel overwhelmed, or if you feel your situation is dire or unique. Your coach will work with you for as long as you need, to get you up the Rich Continuum fast. You also get access to the Rich Habits Coaching Community above.

Rich Habits Business Coaching

Tony has had extensive experience rapidly growing businesses and salvaging companies on the verge of collapse. With this Rich Habit Business Coaching program, you can tap into that experience. Your Rich Habits Coach will develop a customized solution for your business that will help you build a solid financial foundation for future growth. If you're burdened by tax debt, wages, defaulting customers, or unethical partners or staff—there is a solution and Tony has seen it all! With the Rich Habits applied to your business, you will never fall victim of these difficulties again. If you want to develop a financial immune system for your business that will survive the economic ups and downs, and day-to-day challenges, this program is for you.

20

RICH HABITS BOARD GAME

△

The problem with learning and applying Rich Habit is that life takes too long! There are lots of barriers to overcome, for example; the time between paychecks, and the constant barrage of Poor Habits from advertising and media, these reasons and more make it difficult to stay focused on Rich Habits; they slow down learning and delay the repetitive action necessary to making them an actual *habit!*

We need a faster way for a person to practice Rich Habits, to be free to make mistakes without suffering the real pain of financial loss. That is why I developed this board game, and it's fun too!

Due for release in earlier 2018, the game will have 4 versions.

1. **Basic Version** - For mastery of Rich Habits as they apply to personal finances, which can be played by teens and adults.

2. **Kids Version** - To eliminate Poor Habits for good, the leaders of tomorrow need to learn Rich Habits today. This fun and engaging version for young kids, will start them on the path to prosperity before they venture into the wild and crazy economic world.

3. **Business Version** - For business owners, managers and their entire team, whether the business is big or small, this version will help everyone understand and practice Rich Habits for business.

4. **Government Version** - A challenge for our politicians and policymakers to practice Rich Habits at a national level (not sure if this one will be very popular!).

All versions of the game will utilize the same board, only

the playing cards and rules will change.

Visit myrichhabits.com to find out more.

21

RICH HABITS PLEDGE

I find that when we make a promise to another, we tend to try harder to make it stick than we do when we make a promise only to ourselves.

I want you to succeed and become Rich. I know you want that too.

While writing this book, I was trying to think of a way that I could help you directly. Of course, it's not possible for me to help everyone individually, but I started thinking about the concept of getting readers of this book to make a promise to me.

And that is what I want you to do.

I want you to promise me that you will follow the Rich Habits outlined in this book, eliminate your killer debt and become solvent.

You make this promise by taking the "Rich Habits Pledge" at myrichhabits.com by searching for "pledge."

It reads as follows:

The Rich Habits Pledge

As a Rich Rebel, I solemnly pledge to apply the Rich Habits.

1. To be solvent and constantly improve it.

2. To always maintain viability.

3. To follow the Laws of Allocation and allocate my income for the past, present and future.

4. To use debt only for investment purposes only.

5. To always control my finances and never allow a foe to influence my finances.

6. To rise up the Rich Continuum and set an example to others.

7. To spread the word that Rich Habits exist.

I will personally keep track of these pledges and hope to hear of your success at achieving solvency and prosperity.

22
FINAL WORD

I would like to thank you very much for reading this book, and I sincerely hope that it helps improve your financial situation. I would be delighted to hear of your success and any feedback you have. You can submit your success and feedback via the Contact Us page on our website.

As a final word, I want you to truly prosper, which means *to grow stronger; to gain wealth; to have good fortune; to be successful; to succeed*—in the Old Latin sense the word *pro spere* meant to *forward a hope,* and that is my wish for you.

Fly high!

23
RICH HABITS DEFINITIONS AND FORMULAS

Precise definitions for words must exist to ensure clarity and understanding. One of the reasons the world of finance and tax is so confusing and unnecessarily complex is due the constant changing and twisting of keywords. Legal battles are often no more than a battle to change or enforce the *meaning* of words. Therefore, great care has been taken to clearly define the Rich Habit terms, to ensure that you can *apply* these techniques and indeed, make them a habit!

A word of advice: If Rich Habit terms conflict with your own ideas of the word, or even if they conflict with the dictionary definitions, use these Rich Habits definitions instead, for this simple reason—they are workable.

Rich Habits Definitions

Solvent is having more assets than debt; it means being able to pay one's debts and bills in full.

Viable means your income is greater than your expenses.

Rich is being abundantly solvent and viable.

Broke is having no money left over. Zero solvency and barely viable.

Poor is being insolvent and unviable.

Rich Continuum is a continuous sequence or journey from Poor to Rich in which adjacent levels are not perceptibly different from each other, although the extremes are quite distinct and obvious. The main levels are Poor, Broke and Rich.

Assets are anything that has the potential to increase in value or provide an income and can be easily sold and converted to cash.

Investment debt is money borrowed to buy assets that increase in value and/or provide an income.

Killer debt is money owed that is not backed by assets. It includes overdue or unpaid bills.

Debt is what you owe.

Allocate means separating money for a specific purpose and using it only for that purpose.

Money Received is the total amount of money received for a given period, such as a week or month.

Unusable Income is money received that does not belong to you and must be set-aside before any other allocations occur.

True Income is the remainder leftover from Money Received, after Unusable Income has been removed.

Invest is using money to buy something that provides a profit or income or both.

Rich Habits Formulas

Solvency = value of assets less total debt.

True Income = Money Received less Unusable Income.

Viability = True Income is greater than or equal to your allocations.

Poor Habits + Foes = Destitute, misery, heartache, and upset.

Rich Habits + Friends = Prosperity, joy, happiness, fun and love.

24

RICH HABITS & POOR HABITS

These Rich Habits form the basis of everything you need to know to be Rich. The accompanying Poor Habits show you what you must avoid.

The first 6 habits are the most important. The rest are in the order they appeared in the book.

Awareness

The Rich are aware of and practice Rich Habits.

The Poor are ignorant of Rich Habits and practice Poor Habits.

Solvent

The Rich are solvent and constantly improve it.

The Poor tolerate being insolvent.

Viable

The Rich are always viable.

The Poor tolerate being unviable.

Allocate

The Rich always allocate.

The Poor spend without plan.

~

The Rich always know the income required for True Allocation.

The Poor are ignorant of the income needed to allocate and be viable.

Foe Influence

The Rich identify and eliminate foe influence.

The Poor cannot tell the difference between friend or foe and thus suffer.

Money Skills

The Rich know there are two money skills: One is the ability to make money and the other is the ability to control money. The Rich know that control is the most important of the two.

The Poor focus on making money and rarely develop the ability to control it.

Value of Money

The Rich know that the value of money is based solely on an agreement.

The Poor value money based on time.

Money Manipulation

The Rich know that the value of money can be manipulated.

The Poor are oblivious to and victimized by money manipulation.

Inflation

The Rich know that inflation is the devaluation of money and put their money to work to beat inflation.

The Poor are oblivious to and victimized by inflation.

Tax

The Rich know inflation acts like a hidden tax.

The Poor are unknowingly taxed more because of inflation.

~

The Rich focus primarily on making money and legally minimize tax when possible.

The Poor, in an effort to avoid tax, get distracted from making money.

Compounding Interest

The Rich utilize the effect of compounding interest to boost their wealth.

The Poor get trapped into never-ending debt because of compounding interest.

Debt

The Rich use debt to invest (Investment debt).

The Poor use debt to spend (Killer debt).

Education

The Rich know that education in yourself is the best investment you can make.

The Poor rarely invest in themselves.

Learning

The Rich never stop learning.

The Poor think they already know and cease to learn.

Negotiation

The Rich know everything is negotiable.

The Poor compromise.

Financial Control

The Rich are impossible to deceive because they maintain financial control.

The Poor can be easily deceived because they lack any financial control.

Judgement

The Rich separate fact from opinion and use their own judgement.

The Poor confuse facts and opinions and make mistakes, or fail to act.

Responsibility

The Rich teach Rich Habits by example and encourage others to do the same.

The Poor teach Poor Habits by example and think the Rich are lucky.

Proactiveness

The Rich are proactive.

The Poor blame.

Work

The Rich are willing to work hard.

The Poor avoid hard work.

25
ABOUT THE AUTHOR

△

Born in the UK in 1973, Tony Melvin grew up with a passion for business. He founded his first "enterprise" around the age of 10 years old: a car washing business. His younger sister Catherine and friend Julia were the hired help. Tony was the salesman. Despite the business having only one client and lasting only a single day, he never forgot how easy it was to make money solving people's problems.

Since then, Tony has learned the ropes of business and finance from his studies and experience. Over the past 20 years he has travelled Australia and Asia teaching finance and business principles to thousands. As managing director, he helped build the fastest-growing accounting firm in Australia, and during that same period he co-authored three best-selling finance books.

While Tony is a successful business man and investor, he considers himself first and foremost an educator. Considered by many an authority on finance matters, Tony is regularly interviewed and quoted in the press. As a result, Tony is a sought-after speaker.

Today, Tony is focusing his energy on educating people

about the Rich Habits. He believes that everyone can truly prosper with the right knowledge and skills.

For more information or to request Tony as a speaker, visit:

TonyMelvin.com

www.ingramcontent.com/pod-product-compliance
Lightning Source LLC
Chambersburg PA
CBHW021430180326
41458CB00001B/199

* 9 7 8 0 6 9 2 0 5 5 6 1 8 *